SUCCESS

FOREWORD BY BRIAN TRACY

EDITED BY MICHAEL ST. JOHN

Copyright © 2011 by Solomon Brenner

Shark Bite Publishing
1800 Bridgetown Pike
Feasterville, PA 19053

ISBN: 978-0-578-07313-2

CONTENTS

*This book is dedicated to the wonderful
Black Belts of Action Karate
who constantly strive to
exemplify the true martial arts spirit.*

*Secondly, to all of our instructors
who always inspire me and
continue to make a positive impact
on the world.*

Thank you

FOREWORD

Brian Tracy

When I began my career—uneducated, unskilled, and often unemployed—all I could get were jobs that involved labor: washing dishes, construction work, and even digging wells on farms and ranches.

Then I began to ask, "Why is it that some people are more successful than others?" This question changed my life. Since that moment of awareness I have traveled and worked in more than 80 countries. I have started, built, managed or turned around 22 different businesses. I have served as a consultant or trainer for more than five hundred companies, and taught more than two million students and seminar participants. Through all my teaching and studying, one thing I know for sure is that successful people are different than ordinary people.

Successful people are more upbeat and optimistic. Successful people have a burning desire for fulfillment and as a result are more focused on their goals and objectives. If they're not happy with their life situation, they go to work and change it; they don't wait for someone else to come along and do it for them.

I know this to be true because I've dedicated my life to learning what makes successful people successful. In this powerful book by Solomon Brenner, you will read the stories and secrets of people who are truly Black Belts of Success. Solomon is devoted to helping his students reach their full potential and break through their comfort zone. This book will help you do the same.

Put up your tray tables. Put on your seat belts. Get ready to kick some butt! You're about to begin your journey to Black Belt Success!

Good Luck and Hi'ya!

Brian Tracy

CEO, Brian Tracy International

www.BrianTracy.com

MY SUCCESS

Solomon Brenner

There are people in my life who have hurt me. There are people in my life who have helped me. This is the story of how I leaned on, stood with, and grew with the ones who helped me; how I moved beyond the ones who weren't there for me, learned some critical lessons, and found the one true thing that I was working for all along: *success*.

Here are my successes: I run a successful chain of karate schools in the Philadelphia area, Action Karate. I have published my first book, *Black Belt Parenting*, which sold out the first run. I hold seminars in the United States and abroad on goal setting, vision, self-confidence, self-defense, and parenting.

But as with all success stories, this is not just about the determination of one person. This definitely is not about me. No one can do it alone. I certainly couldn't.

And so my success story is really about all of the people who helped make me successful. I hope you can use my story—and the others in this book—to find your own path to success with the people around you. None of those successful people did it alone, and they'll be happy to tell you that.

You may see a bit of yourself in my story—and all of these stories—and realize that you aren't the only one who has had major challenges along the way. I hope you find success even faster than I did, without all the pitfalls along the way. But if you hit the pitfalls, remember you realize that it's not the end. The dream isn't over. It's just a short stop along the way to success.

As you read this book, I think you will begin to understand that all of us have gone through hard times. We may be successful now, but it wasn't always that way. Before I started speaking around the country about self-motivation, before I ran a successful string of karate schools, there were times when I knew I could fail.

It was hard to imagine just a few years ago that my story would be included in a book about success. For a time, my book could have been a Steven King horror story. I decided that failure was not an option!

But no matter what is going on in your life, imagine yourself as a success. Given time and perseverance, things will turn around. It may not be your reality today, but there are people out there who will make sure that it happens. I know it's true, because what happened to me left me wondering if there were any good people out there. I was hurt.

I can assure you that there are good people around you. Identify them. This book is filled with testimonials to the good people out there.

Here is my success story.

I was twenty when I opened my first karate school. I was young and inexperienced, but I had all the motivation in the world. I knew that was what I wanted to do from the time I was fourteen and put on my first gi. I didn't want to do anything else. My parents raised nine children and didn't have the means to help me out, but they did what they could to get my dream going.

I also found an amazing business partner, Jacqueline. We were a great team. She was busy raising two children, but she had the experience, attitude, and charisma necessary to run a business. She put everything she had into it.

Meanwhile, I had the passion for karate and the ideas for encouraging people to commit to it. Sure, I was young. However, even then, I think I was a natural instructor. What I lacked in experience I made up for with energy.

I remember how happy I was to see my first students earn their yellow belts. They got their new belts in a small promotion ceremony—nothing like the extravagant Black Belt Spectaculars that I host nowadays—but at the time it was a major step forward, both for them and for me. I felt that their success was my success. I knew that if I could guide them through the first step from white to yellow belt, I could take anyone from white belt all the way to black belt. Simply, I knew then that I would make it.

But I wasn't done there. I had visions of many successful karate schools run by my best students, spreading the martial arts to as many people as possible. I had visions of a big business, where thousands of people had the opportunity to earn their black belts and learn the exciting things about karate that had changed my life. For a while, I felt unstoppable. And the feeling was infectious.

Some of my first students saw the great life that I had with karate schools and wanted to do the same thing—just as I had hoped. Action Karate opened its second school in 1997.

At the time, I was barely out of college. I went to class during my off time. I studied late at night, knowing that I wanted a degree to go along with my business.

Soon everything was falling into place. Once that second school opened, other people saw that Action Karate could be successful over and over again by simply repeating the system we had set up. Soon, I was constantly talking to potential school owners who saw themselves living a life as a successful proprietor of an Action Karate school.

A year after that second school opened, we had three schools. Five years later, we had thirteen more. Nine years later, we were up to eighteen schools.

Things were going great, to say the least. I hardly had time to catch my breath and think about how successful we were. I was working twelve hours a day, seven days a week, with no time to get sick, and only a very rare day for vacation. I was already living the life I wanted. Working hard, making money, and making people happy. What more could I ask for?

And then one day in November 2003, it all came crashing down. I found out that some of the other school owners were meeting behind my back and had concocted a plan to take the business that I had built away from me. I thought they were my closest friends. I didn't see it coming.

The revelation that they were plotting to secede from Action Karate—out of greed, I am sure—was the biggest shock of my life. I had encouraged them to become part of the business so that they would thrive, and they were earning far more money than they had been making before. I realized that in spite of all I had done to help them experience more success than they could have imagined, it wasn't enough. They got greedy. They decided they didn't need me and set about cutting me out of my business.

So it is clear: I know all too well how damaging it can be to have the wrong people in your inner circle. There I was, happily working with a team of eighteen schools, two owners per school. I spent every waking hour with these people, both professionally and personally. I welcomed them into my home when they had no place to stay. I cut them a break when they didn't have the money. I pushed them when they needed it. I encouraged them to do better.

Some owners were getting complacent and lazy, but happy to get by. I did what I could to encourage them to get better. They didn't always want to work hard. What I realize now is that I shouldn't have let them into my inner circle. I always embraced people who came into my life wanting the same success that I enjoy. I wanted them to be successful. I figured they would all be good people.

Unfortunately, I was so eager for their success that I failed to see their flaws. I only saw the good in all of them, saw how they could improve their lives and be better people. I was wrong. I was betrayed. And then I was sued.

I lost so much money in the ensuing court battle that it didn't matter whether I won. I lost so much momentum that I thought I would never recover. I lost so many friends that it didn't matter whether I was right. I lost my feeling of success.

Eventually, I lost a big chunk of the business, but that turned out to be the best thing that could have happened. Things had to change.

I learned that sometimes you have to get smaller to get bigger. I dropped from eighteen schools to eight, slimming down the business. I acknowledge that there are good things about these people who left, but they weren't the kind of people who should be part of my organization. I have learned that good character is the foundation of a working relationship.

I fell for many of the same trials that many of you face in the uphill battle for success. But I fought hard to forge forward, and you can do the same thing. My business is now stronger, more profitable, and more successful than ever.

Here's how I did it.

I realized that the eight schools that stayed with me were my true partners. I will never forget their loyalty. I know that the people who stuck with me during that rough patch are the ones who are really there for me.

But, with the wind ripped out of my sails, I also needed more than them to forge on. I found the right people. Better people. I started operating with a new sense of discrimination regarding who I would invite in as a friend.

I found that's the key to success.

I started to surround myself with successful people. It doesn't matter how you define success. Define it and then invite people into your life only if they meet those criteria. This cannot just be successful people who are rich or powerful. They have to have integrity and other characteristics that can help propel you forward. For me, those people are the ones who have contributed their success stories in this book.

Perhaps most important on that list is Omar Periu, whom I so admired as a motivational speaker that I began calling him for personal guidance. He became a friend. He understood. He went through similar hard times. You will read about them later.

Despite all of that, he forced me to demand more out of myself.

As I've traveled around and visited many people in many states, I've discovered what I think I always knew to be true. Everyone takes hits on the road to success. I found solace in other people's stories. I am inspired by the plight of others who went through harder times than I did and rebounded bigger and better.

I can accept my flaws and faults because everyone, even the most successful people I know, have flaws. To me, all of the contributors to this book are truly successful. Having a good relationship with each of them makes me a better person. Relationships are paramount to everything. In any business, most opportunities for growth come from forging good connections. In many ways, it's the most important thing you have. Always give back to the relationship. That's why I can't thank my mentors and friends enough for what they have done for me. They can each be called a success and have helped me become a better person, a success.

I love the word success. I love saying it, writing it, thinking about it. Sweet success. It's what everyone wants.

Success is working toward a worthwhile endeavor. If I'm consistently moving forward toward what I want to achieve, I'm successful. My goal is to make one million people successful. That may sound like a lot, but if I work hard every day to make more people successful, I think I can achieve it. And imagine what would happen if they each have that same goal and pass it forward. The influence would be staggering. That's why I wrote this book. I thought it was an opportunity to reach more people and get them on the road to success.

One thing that successful people have in common is actually a sneaker slogan: just do it. I told Omar that I thought I was beaten, and he told me that I just needed to keep going. Just do it. I had that attitude when I first started, and I have used that motto every step of the way.

You want to take that step forward? Just do it. Don't bother reading this book or going to a seminar if you're not going to implement the lessons you learn. Education is nothing if you don't use it. I often meet the owners of other karate schools who are well educated and well versed in the best ways to do business. They do all their homework. At any time, you can ask them the best methods to run a karate school, and they will rattle them off.

Ask them if they're actually doing them, and it's another story. They have all the knowledge in the world, but they don't necessarily have the initiative to use it. The solution is clear: just do it. This is what happened when I wanted to open my own karate school. I had every excuse not to do it. I was young and inexperienced. I needed help. But I knew that if I just did it, everything would fall into place.

That brings me to the next point: stay educated. Now that I've been successful in the karate business and have given dozens of speeches on it, I cannot settle. I cannot be complacent. Although I've reached a point at which I am comfortable, I am not comfortable staying still. I need to keep getting better, or I will lose people on the journey. I won't be able to motivate people if I'm not motivated myself.

After years of training as a martial artist, I recently took up Tang Soo Do with World Champion, Anthony Atkins. Suddenly I was a white belt again, and it was one of the most exciting times in my life. I was doing what I love—karate—but everything was new and different all over again. I worked my way up to black belt and felt like I had accomplished success on another level. I have also begun studying pressure points and Krav Maga, the exciting form of karate used by the Israeli army.

In the karate business, there is no national standard. In the workout industry, you have Bally's and L.A. Fitness that carry their names across the country. In karate, you have you, your name, and your personality to carry the school as far as you can take it. Around the country, there are masters of the martial arts industry, and I try to learn from them. Let your personality take your school to the next level.

But don't just learn your business. Learn about other industries and other businesses and how they do it. If people are impressed with you, it's not because you're the best karate instructor they found. It's because you're the best, period. That's why I read books about people who are successful in other industries and try to learn how they do it. Learn the tricks of CEOs and athletes and inventors—people who have risen to the top of their field. If you want to be great at customer service, be the best. Learn from Disney. Don't just take a vacation there. Try to use it in your business. Don't just say you're the best in your business. Be the best overall. People will compare you to every other experience they've had with FedEx and Verizon and Apple and every other customer service center. And while you may stack up well against some of those, the key is to be better than all of them. Give students confidence in making the right decision to deal with you.

Those tips focus on improving your mental faculties, but taking care of your body is also critical. People instantly recognize a fit person as being confident and focused. There are overweight people who are successful, sure, but they first have to battle the negative image their shape projects. Being in shape will not only make you look confident, but you will feel more confident, knowing that you will not get winded taking the stairs, or injured playing weekend sports. To keep your mind acutely alert, keep challenging your body to see what it can do. By challenging yourself and constantly growing as a person, you will also be the positive person in other people's lives. You could be the inspiration to the next Martial Arts Superstar. But you won't inspire a master unless you first act like one.

There's something called the "Law of the Lid" that explains this. Here's how it works. The leader is the lid. If you are the leader, you are at the top of what your team can accomplish. If you are only a five as a leader, then everyone under you can only be a three. If you are a seven as a leader, the people you lead can be a five or a six. The only way to make them better is to make yourself better. Don't complain that the people around you are inadequate if you're not raising the lid to make room for their progress. If you don't think the people around you are performing to their potential, the first person you should look at is the person in the mirror. You are somehow attracting these people. Don't worry about them. Worry about yourself, and they will follow.

Never say no. The hallmark of wealthy people is they never say no to their own goals. They see success around the corner and they don't talk themselves out of it. They keep pushing until they get it. Set your goals, figure out how to make them happen, and stop telling yourself that you can't do it.

And finally, a word about money: Save it. Save money so that you're financially secure.

The following chapters are from the people who have inspired me to succeed over the years. I know they will do the same for you.

Solomon Brenner is the master instructor and mentor for nine professional martial arts schools in the Philadelphia area. He is sought after internationally for his seminars on character development and goal setting, as well as by other martial arts school owners looking to take their business to the next level. Master Brenner is a seventh degree black belt in American Kenpo and is also the author of Black Belt Parenting: The Art of Raising Children for "Success."

WHEN OPPORTUNITY KNOCKS

Greg Silva

My name is Greg Silva and I am president of United Professionals (UP).UP is one of the world's largest martial arts tuition billing and consulting companies. We represent about one thousand schools in the United States, Canada, and the United Kingdom. In addition to United Professionals, I am also the president of www.getstudents.com, a marketing supply company for martial arts, gymnastic, dance, and fitness facilities, as well as Consulting by Choice, which is a personal success-coaching program for the martial arts industry.

I have authored two books, *The Silva Solution, Building Black Belts from the Inside Out,* and *KICKIN—Coloring projects for inspiring martial artists.* My career in the martial arts began in 1970 while I was taking martial arts lessons at a school in Wethersfield, Connecticut. I arrived for class one day and my instructor said, "Danny quit. Do you want a job teaching?" At the time I was a student at the University of Connecticut, so I had plenty of time in the evenings. I continued teaching for the school until 1973. I also graduated that year. I purchased the school from my instructor, and that's when it all began. At that time, Bruce Lee's movies were box office hits, and the industry was growing quickly. My school became highly profitable within six months of me taking it over. Soon Bruce Lee died, and the movie industry that had fueled interest in the martial arts wasn't there. Students were leaving, and the economy was dragging. I moved to a smaller school and began rethinking the way I was doing business. I became interested in expanding my market to teaching children. I created a new marketing campaign and was soon on the way up again, growing to six locations and almost two thousand active students. I networked with other schools, and my competitive nature took over. I heard stories about a school owner that had six hundred students in a single location. I believed that I had the talent but not the market to achieve similar results, so I sold everything and moved to the sunshine state. Upon arrival, I opened a school in Coral Springs, Florida. I did my due diligence and chose what I considered the perfect town. There were 78,000 people within a two-mile radius with 80 percent of the population in the age bracket that I was targeting. What happened next was remarkable. In three years, I built the largest school in the country with 1340 active students. This success was the catalyst I needed to move to the next level, helping school owners do what I was doing—making a great living doing something for which I had a real passion.

Success is defined many ways, and I am sure you have your definition. However, to clarify what I am referring to in this chapter, I view success as having financial freedom, the ability to help others increase their financial success, and the security that I can choose to stop working yet maintain my life style, making large contributions and life changes in others and my community.

Zig Ziglar says it best, "You can have everything in life you want if you will just help enough other people get what they want." Zig also said ten very important two-letter words: **"If it is to be it is up to me." With that and the help of the Lord, you just can't miss.**

I do believe that I was programmed for success at a very young age. My parents were self-employed in the bakery business when I was growing up. I saw them work long hours and also reap the financial rewards of having their own business. Although they kept telling me not to go into the bakery business, they did teach me that being an entrepreneur was the way to financial independence. Working for yourself allows you to be rewarded for your hard work, and no one except yourself is going to stop you.

My parents began teaching me how to run a business when I was twelve years old. We had a summer home on a lake, and every night my parents and I went out in the yard to collect night crawlers. We had a sign in the front yard, and it was my responsibility to count out the worms, collect the money, and take care of the customers. Being in the bakery business, I knew about a "baker's dozen," and all of my customers got thirteen worms for the price of twelve. I was already wired on the importance of great customer service. "Okay, I got it," I thought at age twelve. "Provide a product in a good location and make sales. Treat the customers nicely, and they will come back for more—I can do this." I believe I only worked for someone else for one year in my entire life. When I was in high school, I worked for an automotive parts store, making deliveries. My father then suggested that I go to a wholesale floral market and buy flowers on Friday and set up a stand on the weekends. I ended up making more in two days than I made all week at the auto store. That was good in high school, but I needed more money in college. I saw an ad for someone to work a hot dog stand in Hartford Connecticut. I worked one day and couldn't believe the money I took in for the owner. I also couldn't believe the small percentage I received for my work. The very next day I asked the owner if he would be interested in selling his truck and business, and all of a sudden, I was a business owner. Here I was, eighteen years old, making $200 a day working 10:00 AM to 2:00 PM. I was hooked on working for myself and never turned back.

Of course, not every day was a good day, and challenges came up; however, my parents drilled into my head that I could do anything I put my mind to. They also would never accept an excuse. After all, according to my mother, I was a Silva, and a Silva can do anything he puts his mind to. Silvas never quit, Silvas are smart, Silvas receive good fortune and so on. I believe that this belief system that my parents instilled in me was the foundation for the thinking that made taking risks and opening businesses easier. I always weigh the up side and down side of opportunities, however, being smart, being lucky, never giving up, and of course, being a Silva was always on my side.

When working with new clients, I try to find out as much as I can about their belief systems and values in order to help them with their businesses. One question I ask them is, "What drives you?" Is it the fear of failure or the thrill of success? I have found both to be keys of success, depending how strong the desire burns inside, although the fear of failure might be a little stronger. I also ask, "Are you a detail person or a big-picture person?" I do find a big difference here. I find that big-picture people usually see success faster, especially if they build a team of detail people around them. I once built a chain of one hundred licensed martial arts schools in less than three years. Within twenty-four months, the company was netting $100,000 a month with zero investment dollars. I had the idea, and my team took care of putting the pieces together. One challenge I face, although some people may see it as an asset, is that I find fun in building a business or project, but soon I want to sell and move to something new. I took over a failing martial arts school a year ago and totally turned the school around. The ride has been fantastic. However, the thrill is gone, and I am ready to build something new. This time I'm not selling, just rebuilding the school into something new, bigger, and better. I did the same with cars and houses. Or at least I did when the housing market was better. My wife says that I have a trading disorder. I think of it as a passion for never-ending improvement.

Opportunity knocks. I love the Toyota commercial in which the cartoon character knocks on the TV screen: "Opportunity here, and I'm knocking." Some people say I'm lucky. I may be, but only because I believe I am. Let me explain. My dad felt that he was lucky and would always find money, and he did. In fact, my parents would walk daily and almost always find money. Were they lucky? Or was it because they thought they were lucky and always kept an eye out for it? I bet they walked looking down, and that's why they found it.

Let me give you a couple of examples. I think this may open your eyes to opportunities and how they may present themselves to you. I was living on the beach in Hillsboro, Florida, and had to go to the store. It was tourist season and the roads were packed. The bridge going over the Inter-coastal leading to the store was stuck. A ten-minute ride took me an hour. While on the other side of the bridge, I drove down some residential streets looking for *For Sale* signs and saw a nice house for sale. When I arrived home, my wife said that someone had knocked on our door and asked it we would consider selling the condo. Well within thirty days we sold them the condo and bought the house. We made $50,000 on the condo and purchased the house for $525,000. The building stage was on (again my favorite part), and we re-did some minor things on the house, including the landscaping. I knew a great real estate agent, and twelve months later I asked him to list our house at $925,000. We sold it three months later for $885,000. That time opportunity literally knocked while I was shopping, and it netted me $425,000. Of course we didn't really plan on moving, and the new buyers wanted to move in right away. We literally moved two streets away and bought our first house for more than a million dollars. That turned into a great opportunity, and we sold that in a year for a great profit.

I am not trying to impress you, but rather impress upon you the importance of how positive thinking or beliefs can make a huge difference in the way you respond to opportunities and risk taking. This is the second time that I have mentioned risk. You can interchange that word with "change" if you want. Many people I consult get frustrated, because they see the success of others and just don't understand why they seem to be stuck in a rut. The stumbling block is usually their resistance to change, because it involves risk, or maybe they have done something before and it just didn't work. In other words, their beliefs are based on what they view as a personal failure. They fail to understand that all people fail, but that doesn't mean all people are failures.

So what is the secret to getting results quickly and jumping on the fast track to success? The easiest is modeling someone else. Simply find someone who is getting the results you want, and do the exact same thing. At least that's what someone told me when I first began building my martial arts school. I was told to find someone with a large martial arts school, visit his school, and do the same thing. I did just that, and when I returned, my mentor asked me what I had learned.

"Not much," I said. "He teaches the same style, but my students are better, my school looks as good, and "my signs are more visible."

My mentor said, "There had to be some difference."

"Well," I said, "the master instructor seemed very organized; he also had a well-trained staff, he looked very professional, and he was a very gracious host." I then got it. When you model someone, you don't necessarily model what they do, you model who they are, what they think, and what they believe.

I got on the phone and asked questions such as, "What books are you reading?" "You are really motivated. Are there certain tapes you recommend?" "What do you do to train your staff?" "Do you use a day planner?" "What is your day like?" To get the same results by modeling, you need to become a different person, or a least a different thinker, not just do different things.

Well, I did it. I read, listened to tapes, and became a professional business person—not just a "karate guy." What happened next took me by surprise and could have brought everything tumbling down, if I had let it. I found my friends and fellow black belts starting to resent me. You would think that everyone would be happy for your success and say, "Good for you." But that's not what happens. I remember listening to one of my tapes—I believe it was by Tom Hopkins—and he said the view from the top is great, but it can be lonely at first.

When I bought my first luxury car, which was a Jaguar, my friends said, "Well, I guess we aren't in the same league anymore." When I bought a house in a gated community, I got comments such as, "Is that so that we won't visit you anymore?" When the martial arts school grew so much that I had to hire an off-duty police officer to monitor the parking lot to keep the kids safe, some of the long-time students weren't happy for me; they were actually upset. That's just human nature. You will soon find that as you surround yourself with more and more positive and successful people, you get more and more support. I recently bought a Bentley and had it delivered to the house. My neighbors came over to take a look, and I must say that everyone was truly happy for me. They know my nature and my vision to help people enjoy lives of success. So maintaining strong character and high values is an important part of the walk you walk. When you choose someone to model, be sure that he has the character that you will be proud to model.

As you experience success, you will attract other people to you. You will be given opportunities to help and mentor others. This is a fantastic opportunity and a responsibility that you shouldn't take lightly. I have been blessed to help several people go from struggling martial artists to millionaires. I have had some of these people turn on me and become competitors of mine, and I have others who are grateful and loyal. Has this spoiled it for others? Have I stopped giving a hand? No, not at all. God has given His children an abundance, and those who realize this and continue to serve others and provide a service or product that enhances people's lives will be blessed.

As you experience more and more success financially and personally, be sure to maintain a balance in your life. Be careful not to sabotage yourself by becoming a workaholic and neglecting family, your faith, or your health. I have a sign in my school that says, "Work Hard, Train Hard—Play Hard; it's all about balance." I like it, because it's a constant reminder for me to put 100 percent into everything I do, whether it is working, exercising, or having fun. Tony Robbins refers to it as the wheel of life. The spoke of a wheel represents different aspects of life, work, family, contribution, faith, health, and etcetera. If your wheel is to run smoothly, all of your spokes must be of equal length. My sign means the same; it's all about balance.

I received this plaque as a gift, and it sums it all up.

Dance as though no one is watching you.
Love as though you have never been hurt.
Sing as though no one can hear you.
Live as though heaven is on earth.

SOLOMON'S WISDOM
Model someone you would be proud to be.

Soon after graduating from UCONN's School of Business, Greg Silva opened his own school, Farmington Kenpo Karate, soon to become East West Karate. It is now East West MMA with approximately 100 affiliate locations in 2010.

His schools were incredibly successful in the 70s and 80s with 6 locations and almost 2000 active students. During this time he advanced his own personal martial arts training and earned his sixth degree black belt under the late Ed Parker. Following Ed Parker's passing, Mr. Silva was promoted to seventh degree by the World Wide Kenpo Karate Association under Joe Palanzo and Huk Planas. His schools were featured several times in local television for their community service and progress as well as in industry magazines.

Mr. Silva soon moved to Florida and opened Coral Springs East West Karate just northwest of Fort Lauderdale. What happened here was totally amazing. Still a student of Ed Parker's, Mr. Silva felt that there were certain shortcomings in the martial arts with regard to teaching children.

He worked with a child psychologist, studying and learning strategies of children, and made some drastic changes in the way martial arts was presented to children. He invented "Teaching Benefits," "Universal Curriculum" and "Phase Curriculum." Students began learning faster, excelling in the physical progress, and within three years over 1300 students were training in a single facility.

Since that time Mr. Silva never slowed down as a martial arts pioneer. He created United Professionals a tuition billing and consulting company, Corner Man Mentoring and Get Students, a company specializing in marketing material unique to martial arts. He has been a regular speaker for the Martial Arts Industry Association as well as the author of The Silva Solutions *Building Black Belts From The Inside Out.* In addition, he is a real estate developer in Arizona where he lives with his wife Jeannie.

You can reach Greg Silva at 954-290-7869 or by mail at 7260 - 37 E Eagle Crest Dr. Mesa AZ 85207.

DEFINE SUCCESS

Tom Callos

Success? Success! Here is my rambling—my diatribe on the subject:

First let me tell you the truth about success.

Okay, the truth is: I do not know what success is. Of course, that is not going to stop me from thinking, talking, or writing about it, because that is the fun! It is the fun of the unknown (as opposed to the "fear"). Seeking success is, in my opinion, a big part of finding and feeling it. It is like writing. The magic comes in the editing (or re-writing) of the writing, and so with success, the magic comes with the re-exploration of the idea of success. Did I mention that I don't know what success is? Good, as I want to make that clear. My definition of success is not necessarily your brand of success, but it might be one contribution from the "village of people" that helps you define what success is going to mean to you.

I am going to fill the next page or two with what I think success is about—and what it is not about—but all of that is only my opinion. There is no fact here. Ask me again in a year, in a month, in a day, and I might give a different answer. Isn't that great? There's no boredom here, and there's a river-like flow to the idea of success. It changes, it adjusts, it floods, it dries up, and it carries with it all sorts of other things. Maybe success is the river we live in.

Success, the Word

The word "success" is like the word "love"; almost everyone defines it differently. I attended an Anthony Robbins (the motivational speaker and author) seminar in the late 1980s, during which Tony asked the audience—more than 800 people—to break into groups of ten and then each come up with a list of five words describing the word "love" in order of importance. Well, at the end of the exercise, not a single group had the same words in the same order. Some groups used words like "hot" and "passion" to define love, while other used words like "commitment" and "patience." The exercise enlightened everyone in the seminar about word use and clear communication. You say, "I love you" and you are thinking about commitment, while I say it and I'm thinking about ... well, let's leave it at that!

Success is that kind of word. One person uses it and is thinking about her finances or sports cars or living in a certain neighborhood, while another is thinking about simplicity or raising happy children or spiritual enlightenment.

Success is something that you use to define yourself, but it's my opinion that far too many people spend way too much time trying to live out other people's definitions of it. Maybe success is a feeling (I think it is), and feelings are most often stimulated or controlled by an individual's viewpoint. It's the way we look at things that determines our feelings of success—or failure. Didn't Tom Edison have a certain viewpoint about success? Didn't the baseball homerun king, Babe Ruth, who struck out so many, many times, have an idea or two about success—a viewpoint? Edison and Ruth had a viewpoint that a thousand "failures" didn't mean they were failing, but for some people a handful of "failures" is a sign (in their own minds) that they "aren't successful." Isn't there a lesson here?

Success, the Notion

Success is a "notion." It does not really exist. If success is a place, it is an ever-changing place; it is a place where just when you think you know it, you find that it has changed since your last visit. Success is like fitness; it is something that takes constant work. You are not a "success" permanently without ongoing effort anymore than you can be fit permanently without effort.

Success in Bite-Sized Chunks

In my mind, the word "success" is so big that it's difficult to get my head around it. To intelligently talk about success, I need to break it down into bite-sized chunks, making a number of individual distinctions. For example, let's address "health success" first; that's an easy one, as I think everyone wants to enjoy optimum heath. With health, you know that you are successful when you are fit, vibrant, and free from injuries and disease.

How about career success? I am successful at my career when it is a joy to do the work and it brings in enough resources to make life comfortable (another ambiguous term).

How about family success? When my family is healthy and well-taken-care of, am I then successful? I think you can be a success with your family but ignore your health (success in one place, failure in another).

Success is achieved in degrees and in manageable, bite-sized chunks. One part of your life can be successful, while another part is not. The key is to strive for balance. A good thing about this idea is that it allows you to isolate certain parts of your life and work on improving them in an incremental fashion so that you don't feel overwhelmed by the big picture.

What Success Is *Not*, for Me

- Success isn't stagnant. I have not "achieved" success;
- I practice things that make me feel successful.
- Success has nothing to do with anything I can acquire.
- Success doesn't wear a name-brand label.
- Success isn't endorsed by a celerity spokesperson, nor is it something I can wear, drive, or put on my wall.
- Success has less to do with money than it does with love.

What Success Is, for Me

- Success is the freedom to choose.
- Success is engaging in creative endeavors.
- Success is when you make a difference for others.
- Success is the achievement of goals that feed your soul.
- Success is in simplicity, not in acquisition.

Success for Others

In 1992, I took on a personal "success" project; I endeavored to hand-write ten letters a day for six months to different people who I thought were successful. I asked each of them about success and for tips that I might share with my students. I received more than five hundred responses. The civil rights activist and legend Rosa Parks sent me a two-page handwritten letter describing her ideas about success. Convicted Watergate conspirator John Erlichman sent me a handwritten letter that described his experience with President Richard Nixon and what he learned from their collective mistakes. Here are some of the ideas from a few noteworthy responses:

Author Leo Buscaglia (1924–1998), a University of Southern California professor known for his lectures on love, wrote to me on December 3, 1992:

Tom, success is all about love. If you want to feel successful, I propose a few end-of-the-day questions (to keep you on track). Here they are:

- *Is anyone a little happier because I came along today?*
- *Did I leave any concrete evidence of my kindness, any sign of my love?*
- *Did I try to think of someone I know in a more positive light?*
- *Did I help someone to feel joy, to laugh, or at least, to smile?*
- *Have I attempted to remove a little of the rust that is corroding my relationship?*
- *Have I gone through the day without fretting over what I do not have—and celebrating the things I do have?*
- *Have I forgiven others for being less than perfect?*
- *Have I forgiven myself?*
- *Have I learned something new about life, living, or love?*

If you are not satisfied with your answers, take heart. Tomorrow you get to start all over again! If you will do it, this is one quiz you can never fail.

Author Joe Hyams, who was also a student of Bruce Lee, responded to my letter on April 6, 1993:

Dear Tom,

*... I would suggest to anyone interested in doing or achieving anything: **Do it!** Don't talk about it, dream about it, or wish for it. **Do it!** In my experience, anything is possible if you start, keep at it, and finish it. This is what success is made of.*

The famous motivational speaker and writer, Norman Vincent Peale (1898–1993), wrote to me on November 19, 1992, a year before his death:

Dear Tom,

I looked up on my office wall when I read your letter, and I saw the photograph of my teacher in Williams Avenue School of Norwood, Ohio, a suburb of Cincinnati, when I was in the fifth grade—a while ago. His name was George Reeves, and he was a very inspiring character of my boyhood days. He was a big man physically, mentally, and spiritually. He taught me a lot about success.

Mr. Reeves would occasionally write on the chalk board the word "CAN'T" as big as he could make it. Then he would turn to the class and say, 'What shall I do now?' He taught us to say in concert, "Knock the T off the can't!" With a smile, he would knock off the T, leaving the word "CAN" clear and distinct. Then he would say, "Let that be a lesson to you, ladies and gentlemen." He always saluted us in that fashion. And he added, "You can if you think you can. So let yourself think you can." When I think about success, I remember Mr. Reeves.

Bestselling author Danielle Steel responded to my query about success on March 18, 1993:

Dear Mr. Callos,

The most important qualities that anyone can have—the key ingredients for success—are determination and discipline. In my opinion, this is imperative. Nothing gets done without persistence and perseverance.

It is essential to believe in yourself, because setbacks are inevitable. If you really want something and work very, very hard for it, chances are good that you will get it. If you sit around and hope for success, probably nothing will happen.

Success Wrap Up

As I wrap up this little essay on what I think about success, I'm thinking about what it would mean if a reader were to take what I had to say to heart. What if someone actually disconnected the term "success" from anything that had to do with buying or acquiring things? Wouldn't that be a breakthrough? He or she would sure save a lot of money! What if someone read this and decided that love, compassion, and doing for others was his or her definition of the word? Wouldn't that be something!

In the end, I believe that success is all about attitude. That's how I'm approaching it in my own life, and I hope that I've been successful in giving you my viewpoint on the subject in a way that helps you with your own definition.

SOLOMON'S WISDOM
Success is always changing and moving. It's not an achievement; it's something you practice. Tomorrow is another day to try again.

Tom Callos is a writer and consultant to the martial arts industry. His work has had a profound impact on the international martial arts community. His bio and portfolio of work may be seen at www.tomcallos.com.

SUCCESS: WHAT DOES IT REALLY MEAN?

Allie Alberigo

When I was asked to write a chapter of this book, I was quite honored. I felt a sense of accomplishment and realized that at some point I must have achieved some sort of success. I was once asked at what age I decided to be a success, and then what was the one thing that made me successful? I can't remember when the spark went off in me that drove me to achieve. The reason why I say *achieve* is because success is sometimes measured based on accomplishments. For an actor, it may be receiving a "Golden Globe," for a musician it may be creating a hit multi-platinum selling album, or for a real estate mogul such as Donald Trump, it may be building bigger and better buildings and creating new things. Whatever your goals and desires, the one unique thing about successful people is that the majority of them continue pushing the envelope and moving forward every day.

If you want to be a millionaire, once you have achieved that goal, you don't just go into a cave and become reclusive; you constantly strive to grow bigger and better. Throughout this chapter I will continually ask, "What is success?" I have heard many examples; some of them are obscure, some monetary, and others basic. Could a mother of a child consider herself a success just for raising a child to be a great person? Of course. How about a husband who provides for his family and works hard every day? Without a doubt, he is a success as well. What are your goals? What are your dreams? What drives you? What does success mean to you?

Going back in my life, I can remember as early as four years old that I had the inherent desire to be something special. I wanted people to see me as being different and unique—nothing like the rest. I always had an undying desire to succeed in all that I did. At an early age, I started playing guitar and singing, and I ended up becoming a performing musician for the next two decades. I rode horses and had my own horse in my back yard. I raced motorcycles and ended up on Team Suzuki in the early 1970s, when racing was a totally different game. During all of this, I found time to be a kid and practice the martial arts.

The interesting thing was that I was not a very scholastic child. In fact, my mom would celebrate if I barely squeaked by with a passing grade. My mom came from an entirely different paradigm—she only went to school until the third grade. She was born in war-torn Europe on the island of Malta. Most of her adolescent life was spent in a bomb shelter built into the rock of a cliff. My dad was always a happy person and worked first as a clerk in a supermarket, only to move on to a career in law enforcement. My dad had a love for toys—boats, cars, motorcycles, and gadgets. I see now that my mom and dad came from two entirely different worlds. Their marriage ended up in divorce and created an entirely different learning experience for me. Being the child of divorce, I was determined to be even more successful. I could see how hard my mother worked to keep the house up and pay the bills, sometimes working two or three jobs per week. It showed me that anything was possible. During this time, my dad and I were a bit distant, but he still did whatever he could to support any of my dreams.

My first goal in life was to be a world-famous rock musician. I actually started learning how to sing and play guitar at around the age of five and continued lessons until I was about fourteen. At the age of ten, I played in a band and started performing at nightclubs—even though I wasn't of legal age to be there, my talent allowed me this opportunity. Throughout my life until the age of twenty-eight, I pursued this career, recording countless demo tapes for record companies, being managed by some shady individuals, and losing tons of money on scams, recordings, and the pursuit of my dream. Although I never did achieve the level of success that I had dreamed of, I did have a pretty successful career in the business, having opened for some of the hottest bands of the 1980s: Cinderella, The Good Rats, Twisted Sister, Iron Maiden, Paul Dianno, Winger, White Lion, Kix, Slaughter, and many more. I was living the life of a rock star.

I decided to make an extreme career change and pursue a life-long love: to open up a martial arts school and become an actor. Throughout my life, I was self-employed, having only worked for two people in my life as an employee. At the age of sixteen, I realized that I needed to make money, and lots of it, in order to fuel my goals to become a musician and pursue all of the things that I loved. So I formed a landscaping company. This first started off with a small lawn mower and a truck, but thrived into a five crew, full-time company with thirty-two employees. The landscaping business was very good to me. I opened my martial arts school as a hobby and as a sideline to my landscape business to keep me active, working over one hundred hours some weeks in both companies combined. I then started recognizing that not only did I love being a martial artist, but I also loved being a school owner. In 1997, I sold my landscaping business and dove headfirst into running my martial arts school full time.

Throughout the writing of this chapter, I look back and almost amaze myself at the things that I have accomplished, but the thrill only lasts so long. Some may say that I have lived the life of someone so much older than a forty-two-year-old man. Then I think of the old clichés and think, "How much time have I wasted? If I knew then what I know now, I would be that much farther along." Knowledge is only of benefit if you can remember the lessons learned; I am a storybook of those lessons. I share and spread the word of all my mistakes, my accomplishments, and my travels every chance I get. I enjoy telling the stories, and many of them are on my Web sites: www.Lininja.com (my martial arts school) and www.takingittothenextlevel.com (my consulting firm).

Without chronologically providing a check-list of things I have done, I will go back to the one thing that ignited the spark, making me what and who I am today. I would have to say that my parents were my guiding force. Their clear defining message was to follow my dreams. I wanted to be a cowboy—they bought me a horse. I wanted to ride motorcycles—for Christmas I got a dirt bike and all the gear that I needed to ride hard and safely. I loved music—my parents converted the garage; my dad bought a truck to transport my equipment; my mom designed and handmade all of my outfits; and five days per week, they tolerated 100 decibel music pouring out of the garage. Never once as I got older did they say, "Allie, go to school and get good grades, because this may not work out." Never once did they say, "Life is not what it appears to be. You are not the kid in a candy store with a choice of anything you want." They applauded, smiled on, and supported all that I did. Never once did my parents make me feel incompetent or unworthy of the dream. Even though I did not come from a wealthy family, I never felt poor. I had all I ever wanted, and my parents were able to provide for me on a very low income.

People, on the other hand, weren't always so kind. Criticism was not my favorite thing, and not until recently did I learn to take criticism well. Now I learn from it, but in my childhood and younger life I took criticism as a challenge. I would fight back with constant vigor to become better and prove the world wrong. My goal was to show everyone that Allie Alberigo would be someone. My fears were the fuel that made me want to become better. As I matured, I turned that into what is known in the Japanese Martial arts as *Shimbumi*, the pursuit of perfection. My goal was always to be the best I can be.

After reading some of my story, have I brought you any closer to an understanding of success? I am the kind of teacher that teaches through stories, allowing people to come to their own conclusion or enlightenment. I believe that life is a series of tests and trials. What have you learned from yours? What are the components of success to you? In what areas of your life do you want to become a success? Are you a mother or father, a husband or wife? Are you an entrepreneur or an employee? Are you a religious person striving for some inner meaning?

I believe that all successful people have a specific character trait that remains constant. This trait is the desire to be something or somebody special; to step away from the crowd; to be more than just average; to move forward, coming one step closer to your dream each day; to share in the theory of *Shibumi*, the constant pursuit of perfection. The difference between a loser and a winner is sometimes only 0.01 of a second. That 0.01 of a second could mean different awards, depending on what race, competition, or Olympic game you are in. Does that mean you are a winner or a loser? In the eyes of the competitors and fans you may be number one, but in your own—I don't think so.

Life is about doing your very best, recognizing your strengths and talents, and following your dreams. As my parents taught me, dreams can easily become reality if you believe. Life is not about always being on top, but rather performing at the top of your game. Life is a series of steps and stumbling blocks. I call all the sticking points and stumbling blocks speed bumps; they are only there to slow you down and force you to take notice of your surroundings. They are a reminder that there is a bigger picture. You are successful as long as you believe that you are something special.

Within the last three years, I became separated from my wife of thirteen years. In my eyes, I had the perfect marriage. We traveled and we were best friends, but I somehow overlooked things that she thought were wrong. I realized that not everyone sees things the same way, no matter how well they communicate. When I explain this to my students, I always use my own, "Shade of Blue" analogy. If you had a color chart with one hundred shades and mixtures of the color blue and each had a number next to it (my ex-wife and I both loved the color blue), my shade would be closer to white, while hers would be much closer to black. Both were blue, but were very different. After understanding this, I realized that success could be drastically different for many people. Again, I ask: what is success to you?

While traveling in Thailand in 2004, I saw people with houses that were no better than the shed in my backyard and realized that happiness is a form of success. In fact, my shed is a townhouse compared to their homes. I saw people who I thought were living a lifestyle that was not far above prison, yet they were happy, loved, and lived very fulfilled lives. To them, success was something totally different.

I will leave you with a few thoughts. Isn't the very breath you take a sign of your success? Isn't the life you live, no matter what, a success? Is your life something special to someone else? Is your role in the world something that you were destined to fulfill? What is your special purpose? Are you doing what you can to be all that you can be with the special qualities that you have? What is it that will make you a success? What does success mean to you?

I have achieved a great deal in my life spiritually, physically, and monetarily. The one thing that shines above all that is most important to me is my daughter Kiara. She is the reason that I continually push so hard and work toward the goals of *Shibumi*. When I look into her eyes, I truly realize that I am a success.

SOLOMON'S WISDOM:

All of Allie's endeavors were supported by family— no matter the outcome. If you have a great support system, success is achievable.

Allie is a business owner of ten corporations, including his five martial arts schools—four in Long Island, NY, and one in Bermuda. He is a published author, poet, and singer/songwriter. He speaks internationally and consults for many business owners in and out of the martial arts. He is an aspiring actor and a producer of industrial, instructional, and theatrical releases, as well as a stunt choreographer and consultant. Allie is also a real estate investor and helps business owners recognize the dream of owning their own business through his consulting business and martial arts consulting company. Allie can be reached through his Web sites at www.lininja.com or www.takingittothenextlevel.com or through his personal e-mail at Renshilininja@aol.com.

DEVELOP THE MINDSET
FOR SUCCESS

Rob Colasanti

I've noticed that all successful martial arts school owners have something special in common. It's not their style, experience, location, IQ, or square footage. It's definitely not how many trophies they've won. It's their mindset.

If you want to be successful, you first have to believe that you can be successful. That's the critical first step. If you train your mind to believe that you will succeed in achieving your goals and you focus on them long and hard enough, you will most likely achieve those goals. As simple as it sounds, that's how it works.

In my recent interviews with Zig Ziglar, Anthony Robbins, and Brian Tracy, we spoke about the Pygmalion Principle, otherwise known as the self-fulfilling prophecy. Basically, we are our own fortunetellers. We end up consciously and subconsciously creating the evidence to support our claims. Ultimately, our thoughts become our actions, and our actions create the quality of our lives. That's why it's so important to develop the right mindset for success.

Here are five powerful tips that will help you fine-tune your mindset and unlock your true potential.

Always Think Positive Thoughts

If you want to be a successful person, you have to be a positive thinker. Always do your best to eliminate negative thoughts from your mind, and find the good in every situation. Negative thinking will only hold you back from reaching your goals and being a healthy, happy, productive person. On this note, look at virtually any highly successful individual, and you will quickly notice that he or she is a positive thinker. The evidence is all around you. See the pattern?

Constantly Feed Your Brain

Your success will only grow to the level that you do. That's why you should always be learning as much as you can from highly successful people. Few things can motivate you more and get you in the success mindset faster than a really good success coach or mentor. These people already are where you want to go. Study their work constantly, and their success mindset will begin to rub off on you.

Believe in Yourself

Enter every situation with a victory mindset and the intent to succeed. You must erase any self-doubt, fear, and uncertainty from your psyche. Focus not on what you're afraid of, but on where you want to go. As we've already discussed, you'll end up creating your own self-fulfilling prophecies: the kind that lead to success. If you do not believe in yourself, your students and staff won't either, and you'll never build the school of your dreams.

Surround Yourself with Winners

If you want to feel and think negatively, then hang around negative people. They'll be sure to grab you by the ankles and pull you right back down to their level every chance they get. On the other hand, success breeds success. The more you associate with winners, the more you'll start to think and act like one. For this reason, I recommend that you create a peer group of winners. Do this, and you'll dramatically increase the rate at which you develop the mindset for success and become a winner.

Think Big, Not Small

Someone once said that if you aim your arrow at a star, you might hit the moon. But if you aim your arrow at the moon, you might only hit an eagle. It's true. That's why highly successful individuals think big. They set their goals high and fish for whales—not guppies. On the other hand, I've found that unsuccessful people typically think small. They're happy to just get by. So usually, that's all they end up with—mediocre results, and only enough "success" to just get by. You want and deserve better than that for yourself, don't you?

Now, I typically do not speak in absolutes. But in this case I will. Unless you develop the right mindset, you will never become highly successful in the martial arts business, or in any business for that matter. The bottom line is that you can't think like a loser and expect to be a winner. *Simply put, having the right mindset is a prerequisite for success!*

SOLOMON'S WISDOM
Have a positive mindset!

Rob Colasanti is the president of NAPMA, the author of How to Build the Martial Arts School of Your Dreams, an ACMA certified instructor, and a popular speaker on the subject of martial arts school operations

Rob Colasanti has emerged as the leader of the next generation of martial arts professionals and is poised to become one of the primary forces to propel the industry to an even greater position of public prominence and respect.

Born in Queens, New York, during April 1970, Mr. Colasanti's passion for the martial arts began at the age of fourteen; his family was now living in St. Petersburg, Florida. He borrowed his grandfather's lawn mower to earn the money for his tuition at John Graden's USA Karate.

By the rank of Green Belt, Mr. Colasanti had already joined the school's professional staff. During the next twelve years, he earned his Third-Degree Black Belt in American Taekwondo, and advanced as a professional, becoming the school's highly successful program director, a chief instructor, and a popular private-lessons teacher.

Young men grow to have other passions for learning and Mr. Colasanti's personal goals included medical school. In fact, he graduated from the University of South Florida with a B.S. in Biology in preparation to become a physician.

Eventually one passion superseded all others and Mr. Colasanti discovered his future during 1995, when he accepted a one-night-a-week position as the program director (the first official employee) of the newly founded National Association of Professional Martial Artists (NAPMA). It started as a grass-roots organization, without significant capitalization, and operated from a spare bedroom in

John Graden's home. John Graden was the founder of NAPMA and Martial Arts Professional Magazine.

Mr. Colasanti's professionalism and leadership skills developed as NAPMA quickly became the world's largest professional martial arts association.

For his significant contribution to NAPMA, Mr. Colasanti was named vice-president during 1998. His new leadership role and vast accomplishments earned him the respect of his peers and a promotion to president of the association and Martial Arts Professional Magazine, the organization's official monthly publication, during December 2001.

The young president's task was formidable, but by 2005, NAPMA's 10th anniversary, his leadership had not only preserved NAPMA's original position as the world's leading professional martial arts association, but also inspired the organization to surpass previous monthly enrollment levels and prestige.

He is the author of the book, What I've Learned and its 2006, updated version, How To Build the Martial Arts School of Your Dreams. Both have been widely read by young instructors as well as many other industry leaders.

Also, he is an American Council on Martial Arts (ACMA) certified instructor.

Rob Colasanti has broadened his leadership role as the one professional responsible for introducing the leading minds of business, sales, marketing, and personal development to the martial arts industry.

His comprehensive interviews with brilliant and successful individuals such as Jackie Chan, Zig Ziglar, Anthony Robbins, Brian Tracy, Jay Abraham, Tom Hopkins, Jean Claude Van Damme, Matt Furey, Chet Holmes, Dr. Paul Hartunian, Lee Milteer, Tim "4-Hour Workweek" Ferris, Bill Amelio of Dell Computers, and many others have been hailed by thousands.

His up-close and personal interviews with fight legends and martial arts business leaders have motivated and inspired countless martial arts instructors and school owners throughout the world.

Colasanti's interviews are widely considered to be the finest and most comprehensive interviews in the history of the martial arts. Some such interviews were with Kathy Long, Grandmaster Jhoon Rhee, Steve LaVallee, Tommy Lee, Bill "Superfoot" Wallace, Billy Blanks, Evander Holyfield, Joe Lewis, Benny "The Jet" Urquidez, Jeff Smith, Paul Garcia, Joe Corley, Greg Sliva, Joon P. Choi, Rick Bell, Gene LeBell, etc.

Now, every martial arts professional is able to strive for even greater professional and personal goals, which they might have previously thought unattainable.

Mr. Colasanti has also become recognized as the goodwill ambassador of the martial arts.

He is a much sought-after and popular speaker on school operations, industry trends, and broad business concepts that apply directly to all martial arts professionals.

During his career, he has had the honor of being interviewed by all kinds of media outlets ranging from CNN to Time Magazine and continues to make himself available when it comes to spreading the good word about the benefits of martial arts training.

Also, he is able to share his insights as a teacher within the intimate setting of the seminar as well as a motivational speaker to large banquet audiences at major industry conventions and events.

As of September 2008, Mr. Colasanti has not been president of NAPMA. However, his passion for improving the standards within the martial arts industry never wanes.

Mr. Colasanti's generation of martial arts professionals is writing the next chapter of the modern history of the industry, and the story of Mr. Colasanti's leadership and influence are destined to fill many pages.

You can reach Mr. Colasanti at robcolasanti1@gmail.com or http://robcolasanti.com/.

PASSION: THE WAY TO YOUR OWN SUCCESS STORY

Michael Chaturantabut

Mr. B,

It means a lot to me that we've been able to continue our friendship over this many years, so I want my contribution to be worthwhile. As you'll see, what I've ended up with is nothing close to what I started with, as I probably would have had ten or more pages to send. I've condensed it into just a few, not purposely, but it just turned out that way. I had to stop worrying about the number of pages, what was enough, and what was too much, and stop trying to evaluate this based on the volume of content that I was writing. I guess it is in sync with my mantra these days: less is more. I want to thank you for giving me this opportunity. This was a great exercise for me as I was able to take some time to reflect on

my life, which has brought more clarity to my mission as I move forward in my pursuits. I hope my contribution is relevant in the scope of your book, as I've really had to shovel off many layers in order to get to the stuff that really makes any sense to me. I've tried to just get to the point and say my piece, but if it comes across a little too abstract, then I'll defer to my "actor" self, blame it on moving back to L.A., and say that I should have written this last year while living in N.Y.C. or hold off the presses until we move back to N.Y.C. I miss the city; it's such a great city! I'll keep my fingers crossed that your editor doesn't toss this one aside and exclude it from the final print!"
Mike Chat

Success. It's all relative. Typically, those who define success in terms of wealth, positions, and honors are still in pursuit of them. Those who have already achieved these tend to define success in terms of happiness. Those who have it all say success is finding a balance between career, personal life, family, leisure, etcetera. You've read all of the books and have heard all the motivational speakers out there say the same things. At this point, although I have achieved success in my life, my success story is still being written—I'm living the dream—my dream—loving the highpoints and struggling through the low points. What's so great is that we are like writers developing our own screenplays. We get to decide who the characters are, what the plot is, and how we want the story to end. Sometimes we bring on writing partners to add elements that complement our writing style. It's all the twists and turns that we get to experience as we go along that make it exciting. To get to the end you just have to do the work—with many, many revisions along the way—but we are never really finished as we always find more work to be done. That's how a great screenplay is developed. Then in filming it, changes are often made on set, unrehearsed on the spur of the moment, and you just have to go with it.

What I do know is that success is relative to your current situation, and the way you view success will constantly change. The way I see it is that true happiness is what lies on the other side of the door. There are countless doors that present options and opportunities. The key is finding the right door for you. Once you find the right door, you just have to open it and walk through. You can achieve immediate happiness by finding something you truly love and doing it every day.

For me, this begins with passion. This one word sums it up. Why? Because it is the root, the base from which we live to achieve our ultimate goal. Yes, ultimately, we all have the same goal: happiness. We do things, because ultimately, we believe they will make us happy. If happiness is not your ultimate goal, there are professionals you can speak to about that (I like to think in terms of the end goal, so I know where it is that I'm going). So, if true happiness is what you seek, then passion must be the base from which you start. Passion = Happiness. No passion, no happiness. You cannot say that you are truly happy if you sort of like what you do. If you don't love it, you don't love it. You've gotta love it! If you don't, you won't truly be fulfilled. You'll always want more or seek something different, or you'll settle for less and justify why you've had to compromise.

Passion: *Gotta* have it, *gotta* love it ("It" being anything you want to pursue)! If you don't have *it*, find it. If you can't find it, search the ends of the earth for it, because it's all worth it. Those who don't find it, regret it, long for it, and—worse case—give up on it. If you don't love it, then you don't love it; move on.

Martial arts is *my* passion. Okay, I've got "it." I love it. I pursue it. I indulge in it. It makes me happy just thinking about it. I loved it before I knew that I could even win any awards, and I still love it after retiring from fourteen years of competition. I just love it, all of it. I found it when I was four years old, watching those cheesy voice-dubbed kung-fu films.

I want to say, "So my advice to you is ...," but I'm not giving advice; don't take it that way, because I don't have the answers, and my success story is still being written, remember? They say actions speak louder than words, so most ask how and what successful people do. What I find more interesting is not what successful people do, but rather their underlying motivations for why they do them. Therein lies the clue that we can all learn from and take with us.

I love what I do, and what I do defines who I am. I do what is right to better others' lives and the world we live in. What I do has meaning and impact, and it is worthwhile. Less is more—this is how I maintain balance. What I am saying is, long after I pass, this is how I will be remembered. How do I know? I've had this passion all my life, and it is who I am and what I live and work for every day. So, what is your passion?

My wife, McKenzie, and I met Ms. Jacque and Mr. Brenner over ten years ago when they were getting ready to open their third school. What we all want to hear is a great "story." We all had the same passion, yet we journeyed down much different paths. In the end, we'll all have our "story" to tell or one that will be told. If not for any other reason, we might as well make it an exciting one! Oh yes, the more hardships, and, of course, heartache, the better! We all love to see people struggle, hit rock bottom, and then pull through in the end, don't we? I assure you that Ms. Jackie and Mr. Brenner's Action Karate screenplay will be a riveting one! A true underdog story, with great characters and *Asah Shark* merchandising!

As for me, you have my character background and description, but the script is still being worked on, so you'll have to wait until the film comes out to get the rest! It will definitely have all the right elements with lots and lots of drama! You can always hire someone to write your screenplay for you ... but that's not very creative, now is it? Don't be afraid to do the work. Live it, love it, demand it! Good luck! *Asah!*

Known as the Tony Hawk of martial arts, Mike Chat is a seven-time World Champion, former Blue Power Ranger and creator of the XMA, Xtreme Martial Arts Performance Training Program. With over 750 licensed XMA facilities worldwide, XMA World Headquarters flagship state-of-the-art training facility in North Hollywood, CA, Mike Chat has also trained and mentored over fifty World Champions and celebrities like Taylor Lautner, Jaden & Willow Smith, Usher, and Apl.de.ap-Black Eyed Peas.
Contact Info:
XMA WORLD HEADQUARTERS
NoHo Arts District
5140 Lankershim Blvd
North Hollywood, CA 91601
Direct: 818-980-9962
e-mail: info@xmahq.com
Web site: www.xmahq.com

SUCCESS IN THE LITTLE THINGS

Master Bill Clark

Success for me is a daily challenge. It's moment by moment and action by action. It's not a big picture of your whole life. If the last ten things I attempted were successes, then today is a successful day. It's a daily challenge, because the next day something new will come up, and there will be new things to accomplish. You have to know the desired outcome of any action or any encounter with another person. If you know the outcome you want, you can judge whether it was a success or not. I don't go into anything unless I know what I want to get out of it.

Success is a work in progress; everything lends itself to a win or a loss. If my schedule is to get up at 6:00 AM, I either win that battle or lose it. Success to me is meeting the daily challenge of everything being in the proper direction. People tend to apply the word success to big things, but it applies to every action, even—and sometimes especially—the little things. If you always focus on the little, the big takes care of itself.

The first step to achieving success is having a vision of the type of leadership you're going to exhibit. You've got to know what you're trying to accomplish and then take responsibility for every aspect and every action of it as well as the outcome that results from it. You have to understand what you can and cannot control, and control the things you can.

Your own thoughts are one thing you can control. Other people can't control what you think; that depends on you. You decide how much you're going to let others influence the way you think, and you decide what you think about yourself. People tend to judge what they can or can't do without even trying. You don't know what you are capable of. You've got to control the desire to judge yourself. If you think you can't do something before you even try, then what hope do you have of succeeding? My martial arts training changed my whole life. It removed limits on what life can be and taught me how to live life to the max.

I was taught that to be a successful person, I must be prepared to lead, follow, and stand alone. I would love to surround myself with successful people, but sometimes you have to accept people for who they are. This may mean helping them in the direction I want them to go. It's important to help those around you.

I have had many failures. Some have been daily, while others have taken time to recognize. You have to keep moving on with your losses and successes, whether at business, in a relationship, or on a diet. You have to make a decision to change, and in order to do that you have to recognize your failure. All people fail and all people win. What's important is that you move on.

People keep chasing the same idea. Don't let it get you down.

Your vision can sometimes be unclear. Don't believe that something is destined to fail. When I fail, I analyze what I could have done differently. Then I do something differently, or I do the same thing a different way. Don't blame yourself. Success or failure hasn't changed you, because your possibilities are growing every day. Don't fixate on a success or failure. It's not about the destination but the journey.

Success doesn't change anything. Sometimes when people reach a goal, they expect things to change and then are let down. Even with success, more challenges arise. If you earn money, you have to work to keep it or make it grow. If you win a fight, you have to work to stay in shape so that you can win your next fight. Today is a direction, not a destination.

Successful people are always happy. In any and every area of life, successful people have two things: vision and happiness. The hardest part of achieving success is remembering:

To keep your vision

There are lots of things that occur every day that can interfere with your vision. Without that vision, however, you're not going to get very far. Remember what it is that you set out to accomplish, and don't let the daily failures or successes deter you from that.

That every act has consequences

If you keep your vision, you might be able to foresee these consequences, but even when you do, you have to be able to follow through with what you started, be a good leader, and take responsibility for every action.

When you fail, you have to realize that you can't live in the past. There may be a perception that something you have done in the past was successful, but I think you miss the boat when you judge on the past. I am tested every day. At the end of the day, I look back and think, "Was it a success?" Just for five minutes, I reflect on all of my activities. There are no guarantees for tomorrow. Keep a big vision of what life can bring, and always display a willingness to change. To be successful, everyone must lead with confidence.

Recommended books:
Atlas Shrugged, by Ayn Rand
The Science of Being Rich, by Wallace D. Wattles

SOLOMON'S WISDOM
Success happens in little increments. At the end of each day, reflect on the small success accomplished.

Chief Master Clark, an Eighth Degree Black Belt, is an innovator of martial arts teaching, competition, and success techniques. His forty years of experience has allowed him to be a mentor for thousands of students, instructors, and masters. His most recent accomplishment is the creation of the Warrior X-Fit fitness program,which is developing a national and world-wide following. www.wxfit.com
To contact Chief Master Clark:
srmaster@aol.com
Karate America
1400 Millcoe Rd, Jacksonville, FL 32225
904-724-2100

TAKE CARE OF THE DAYS, AND THE YEARS TAKE CARE OF THEMSELVES

Dave Kovar

Over the years, I have had the fortunate privilege to meet and be mentored by several amazing people. At first glance, these people seemed to have little in common with each other. At a deeper level, though, I saw a common thread that linked them all together. Every one of my mentors, to a "T," has developed the habit of consistently performing well over time. They have either consciously or unconsciously internalized the old saying that goes, "Take care of the days, and the years take care of themselves." This quote is as true today as when it was originally written. The concept is so simple that it is often overlooked or dismissed in search of something more profound or complicated.

The truth is that successful people are more likely to under-stand the importance of developing positive daily rituals. They will generally refer to the fact that long-term success can be directly related to the number of positive rituals that an individual has developed.

I have learned that if I am constantly mindful of my daily routines, I stay more productive, more "in the zone."

How are your rituals? A good exercise is to analyze your day, from start to finish. What is your routine? When do you wake up? What do you eat for breakfast? What books do you read? Do you exercise? Once you've done this for a day, or better yet, a week, go back and decide whether what you are doing is what you should be doing. If it is, keep going. If not, what can you do differently?

Let's imagine that your morning ritual is as follows: Wake up late, rush out the door without breakfast, then grab a donut on the way to the office while listening to talk radio. How will this one ritual affect your life if it is repeated over the course of ten years?

Now let's imagine instead that your morning ritual is to wake up early, enjoy a tall glass of water, have a brisk workout, and be back home in time to read some positive literature while enjoying a nutritious breakfast. How will this one ritual affect your life if it is repeated over the course of the same ten years? Physically, will you look different? Emotionally, will you feel different? Professionally, where will you be? Spiritually, how centered will you be?

Chances are, you can see how different your life will be by just developing a positive morning ritual. Now, let's magnify this concept by imagining a day ruled by positive rituals. What would it look like?

You might consider writing out, in detail, your ideal day. When will you exercise? What will you read? What will you eat? With whom will you spend time? Where will you live? How will you treat the people around you? The more details, the better. When you are done, read it daily, and do your best to make your perfect day become a reality.

To help figure out what goes into the making of a perfect day, let's discuss some effective strategies that might be helpful.

Develop World-Class Relationships

Simply stated, nothing is more important for success and happiness in our lifetime than our relationships. However, with that said, everyone experiences "stinking thinking" from time to time, some more often than others. Here are a few helpful hints designed to keep you on track, starting with a list of things that you *shouldn't do* when interacting with others, and followed by a list of things that you *should* do.

Ten Don'ts Of Interpersonal Relationships

1.**Don't Argue**. Logic and emotion are like oil and water; they don't mix. Generally speaking, when people argue, they become emotional and don't think clearly. As your emotions become heightened, the likelihood of saying or doing something that you might regret later increases dramatically. Also remember that winning an argument does little to win respect or friendship.

2.**Don't Blame**. When you point the finger at someone else, three fingers point back at you. Blaming others generally means that you are a reactive person, someone who's unwilling to be held accountable for your actions. Blaming others puts your emphasis and thought process on problems, not solutions.

3.**Don't Criticize**. It is one thing to be constructively helpful and another to be unconstructively critical. The quickest way to kill morale is to criticize those on your team.

4.**Don't Prejudge**. Unfortunately, it is natural and very easy to get in the habit of showing certain prejudices; however, it is a terrible habit to have. First, it is a waste of energy. Every moment spent judging others is a moment not spent believing in yourself. Second, when you prejudge others, you're probably wrong as often as you're right; therefore, you are going to miss out on a lot of potentially great relationships.

5.**Don't Be Sarcastic**. Although being cleverly sarcastic is often considered a sign of intelligence, it rarely serves any positive function. More often, sarcasm only demoralizes and belittles the person toward whom it is directed. Remember, "Please," "Thank You," and "May I" said sarcastically are no longer the magic words.

6.**Don't Humiliate**. The absolute quickest way to create resentment and friction is to humiliate someone, especially if you do it in public. Usually, the only person you should make the object of your jokes is yourself. People who enjoy humiliating others usually have a low self-image and try to make themselves feel bigger by knocking others down.

7.**Don't Be Condescending**. A condescending person speaks down to those around them. It is as though their worth is greater than that of others. The only function it serves is to alienate those around you. Watch your tonality, and try to keep yourself from appearing "holier than thou."

8.**Don't Hold A Grudge**. Everybody makes mistakes; some people make them more often than others. But when you hold a grudge toward others, you give them power over you. You are still letting them control you emotionally. Remember, "Small minds hold grudges; big minds forgive and move on."

9.**Don't Be Easily Offended**. How easily someone gets offended is in direct relation to their level of emotional intelligence. Give people the benefit of the doubt, and assume that whatever questionable thing they said was not meant to be taken in a negative way. When it is apparent that an insult has been directed your way, just don't accept it. Remember the phrase that most of us learned as kids: "I'm rubber, you're glue, whatever you say bounces off me and sticks to you."

10.**Don't Take All The Credit**. Nothing is more frustrating than when a team works hard and has some great success, only to have one person say, "I did it." Build up your team by giving as much credit as possible to those around you.

Ten Dos Of Interpersonal Relationships

1.**Be Loyal to Those Not Present.** No one likes to be talked about behind his back, and you should not tolerate people talking badly about others in your presence.

2.**Do More Than Your Fair Share.** We all appreciate working with someone who doesn't say, "That's not my job." Develop a reputation for being somcone who will do "whatever it takes" to get the job done.

3.**Be Dependable.** Get in the habit of being where you are supposed to be, when you are supposed to be there, and ready to do the job.

4.**Pick Your Battles.** The Pope says, "See everything, overlook a lot, correct a little." If you always have to be right, people will tend to resent you and be resistant to your ideas.

5.Put Your Game Face On. We all have personal challenges that we deal with on a regular basis, but when you get to work, leave them at the door.

When having a disagreement with someone, keep these suggestions in mind:

6.Be Flexible. Sometimes it is okay to do it someone else's way.

7.Have a Solution in Mind. Go into the discussion with a potential solution in which the other person may see value, but be flexible and willing to adjust.

8.Try to See the Other Person's Viewpoint before Expressing Your Own(Seek First to Understand and Then to Be Understood). This is important, because people can sense when you are trying to understand how they feel and are therefore much more receptive to understanding your position. Secondly, you might see the validity of what they are doing.

9.Let the Little Things Go. Avoid bringing up unrelated issues that are not affecting the desired outcome. Constantly finding fault tends to make people defensive and never helps to resolve anything.

10.Resist the Temptation to Argue. If you are not sure what to say or how to respond, say nothing.

II. Live the Martial Artist's Lifestyle

Being a martial artist means different things to different people. First and foremost, it means exemplifying the martial arts spirit. A martial artist is someone who is confident without being cocky and, at the same time, calm without being a pushover. He is aware of his surroundings. Her posture is straight and her voice is clear. He practices courage on a regular basis by doing the right thing, regardless of consequences. A martial artist lives each day to the fullest and does his or her best to remain present, focused and 100 percent committed to the task at hand.

Make a list of your strengths as a martial artist. Included in this list should be strengths relating to fitness, nutrition, and sleeping habits. Maintaining a high level of health is critical to being a quality martial artist.

Next, make a list of things that you need to improve upon in order to become a better martial artist. Include in this list all of your weaknesses relating to fitness, nutrition, and sleeping habits. Of course, include aspects of your martial arts training that you need to work on improving as well.

III. Be Proactive

One of the single most important qualities of a successful person, regardless of their profession, is to be proactive. To be proactive means to be solution-oriented. When challenges arise, a successful person seeks out a solution, keeping in mind the people it will affect and the consequences of the various solutions. Many people find themselves lamenting the situation with, "If I hadn't done this," or, "If only he or she had not done that." A successful person focuses on the situation at hand and how to find a positive resolution. Finding the right solution frequently means knowing who to speak to in order to gain insight. A successful person also shares his or her knowledge about how to be proactive, exercise sound judgment, and seek additional insight when needed. The first step to developing a proactive mindset is to look at prior challenges that you have successfully overcome and actually benefited from. Keep a positive mindset and stay focused on the solutions that provide the greatest benefit.

Start by assessing how proactive you are presently. If you are very proactive, then maintaining your current level should be easy. However, if you find that you have not been very proactive, then this section is critical to you.

You might consider taking a look at your current vocabulary. How often do you use words such as "can't," "must," "have to" and "problem"? These words used in the wrong context tend to limit your ability to become proactive, because they instill a sense that things are out of your control. In reality, the reverse is always true. You can't always control the environment around you, but you can always control how you respond to that environment, which will significantly influence the end result. Using the right words and having the right mindset go together. Instead of saying, "There is a problem," say, "There is a challenge." Remember, the kanji in Chinese for "crisis" is the same as "opportunity." Using the word "challenge" suggests an entirely different situation than does using the word "problem." The next time you find yourself saying "can't," replace it with "I prefer not to because ...."

Once you've taken a look at your vocabulary and begin to make it more positive, then you can start taking a more proactive approach to challenges when they arise. It is important to train yourself to become solution-oriented.

IV. Constantly Refine Your Communication Skills

The ability to communicate in an effective manner is an incredibly important part of success. Here are three important keys that go into developing good communication skills:

1.Be a Good Listener
To start with, there is nothing more important in communication than learning to listen. In his book, *The Seven Habits of Highly Successful People*, Stephen Covey sums it up this way: "Seek first to understand and then to be understood." Most successful people listen before deciding what to say. This allows you

to clearly understand the situation from more than just your own perspective, enabling you to establish a better answer. Of equal importance, a person who feels that her ideas have been heard is always more receptive to the thoughts of the person who invested the time and energy to listen to them.

In every interaction that you have, try to become a good listener. Make sure to look the person in the eye, sincerely listen to his comments, and then ask him questions about what he said. This is something that *everyone* has to work on regularly. We all find ourselves getting busy, and the first thing that suffers is listening. *Never* be too busy to listen.

2.Constantly Practice Your Ability to Develop Rapport

You can practice developing rapport with people by remembering to be responsive to their physiology, tonality, and facial expression. The easiest way to develop rapport with someone is to just simply be sincerely interested in what they have to say. Finally, it is important to remember that we all communicate to each other on many different levels: how we dress, our personal hygiene, how we carry ourselves, what we say, and how we say it are all parts of the message that we send out. Is the message you're sending out about yourself congruent with the message you want to be sending out about yourself?

3.Use Your Influence, Not Your Authority

When communicating with those over whom you have authority, it is important to remember that people generally do not like to be told what to do but are usually willing to help when asked. When people are aware that a leader has authority and does not use it unless it is absolutely necessary, they appreciate being asked and not told even more. Using influence rather than authority, when possible, is always a better choice in working with people.

V. Strive To Make Things Better

One of my favorite phrases is, "Be happy, but not satisfied." There are going to be some periods of time when it will be easy to be happy. Even during these periods, however, it is important to not be totally satisfied. Remember, to be a champion, you have to fight like a challenger. While things are good, a successful person will be preparing himself or herself to succeed during the down times that will certainly occur. Your mindset should be that you are happy with your performance, but not satisfied. You should be continuously searching to determine what things you can do to keep yourself strong.

There are certainly going to be days or weeks or months in which nothing seems to be going right. In times like these, you will be hard pressed to find things to be happy about. Remember, unhappiness leads to disenchantment. Your mood affects the mood of the people around you. When things aren't going the way you want, it is important to remember to keep a positive "happy but not satisfied" attitude. Focus on the solutions to your challenges without lamenting the challenges themselves. Have the right mindset, and do whatever it takes to get back on track.

VI. Always Remember, You Control Your Destiny

In closing, there is nothing more important than remembering that you are in control of your success. If something isn't working, change it.

Your actions have a direct effect on your overall success. You have chosen a profession that enriches the lives of others in a very powerful way. Be mindful of that responsibility every morning, and take pride in knowing it. Always do your best. Never do things because you have to; do them because you want to.

You might consider starting each morning by asking yourself the following four questions:

What am I most proud of?

What am I most excited about?

What am I most happy about?

What am I most grateful for?

Asking these questions in a fully engaged manner really helps to kick start your day and keep your attitude positive. When your attitude is good, there is nothing you can't accomplish. When your attitude is bad, everything is a challenge rather than an opportunity.

Finally, end each day by asking yourself the following two questions:

What did I learn today?

How did I contribute today?

Asking yourself these questions every evening will help you consider and retain the things you learned that day. This makes you less likely to need to learn the same lesson another day.

SOLOMON'S WISDOM:
Consistently perform well over time.

Brothers Dave and Tim Kovar own and operate a chain of successful martial arts schools. Additionally, they founded Pro-Mac (Professional Martial Arts College), dedicated to helping martial artists become professionals in Business Management, Mat Mastery, Sales Mastery, Wealth Management, and Cutting-Edge Classroom Concepts. Contact them at promac@kovars.com or by calling MAIA at (866) 626-6226.

LOVE WHAT YOU DO, SUCCEED AT WHAT YOU LOVE

John Hackleman

For me, success is being able to do what I love and being comfortable doing it, whether that means financial security, security in my career, or just comfort with my overall lifestyle. Because I have that, I get to wake up every day and figure out ways to do what I love and ways to make it—my art, my people, my students, my life—even better. Even if you do what you love as a hobby, it can still be your success. I am fortunate that my hobby is my passion and my career.

To be successful, you have to find your passion, throw it up on a wall, focus on it, and go to it. Do whatever it takes to reach it, and let the chips fall where they may. In other words, do what you love and make everything else in your life fall into place, as opposed to making everything fall into place and then trying to find the time and energy to do what you love. What successful people do benefits others and contributes to the overall good. Make sure that what you're doing not only makes you feel happy and content, but also helps others. As a martial artist, that might be teaching others; as a painter it could mean producing art that makes people happy; as a masseuse it's giving people a massage to make them feel good. It's whatever success means to you.

I am a big believer in surrounding yourself with successful people—people more successful than you. Choose to surround yourself with successful people, because they give more and have bigger hearts. You are not an island. I surround myself with friends and business partners. I have no problem accepting help or helping others.

When I opened my first gym, my financial partner bailed on me. It was a hard thing to take, but I wasn't afraid to ask for help to get through it. I worked the desk with only one junior instructor who worked for free until I got the business off the ground. He did it without wanting anything in return.

I don't deal with failure too well. I can deal with little failures, but on the other hand, relationship and family failures tear me up. I whine and cry. When I fail in business, I call Mike Metzger, Tony Robbins, Frank Silverman—close friends who can help me, even when I am emotional. Chuck Liddell is my close friend and mentor. We share a synergistic relationship, constantly helping each other out. I helped Chuck to the top, and he pulled me up with him. When people want to fight, they come to me; when I need help, I know I can go to others.

I am somewhat of a fatalist. That is usually my starting point when I set out to do something. I gain momentum and then get angry when something doesn't work. But I have the determination to keep pushing, failing, and then trying again, just like in a fight. I have lost fights, but this has helped me to become a better fighter. I don't repeat mistakes; I learn from them.

There are many obstacles that could stand between you and success: fear of failing, believing that you're not good enough, laziness, stupidity, not delegating, not accepting help, having no clear target, having no focus, or even drugs and alcohol. You have to work to keep your passion alive and your vision clear in order to avoid these things. It is your determination that will get you over these hurtles. Failing is a part of success. The important part is that you learn from that failure and don't make the same mistakes again. If you don't believe in yourself, no one will. You have to believe that you can be a success and do whatever it takes to reach that goal. Asking for or accepting help can be really hard for some people, but sometimes it is necessary to help get you where you need to be. There is no shame in asking for help.

The most difficult part of success was the road that took me from being unsuccessful when I started out, to being successful. Unless you are born with a silver spoon in your mouth, it can be really difficult to work through those beginning years to get to success. You have to remember that success is a gradual process. It isn't going to happen overnight. It's the little things you do from day to day that make the biggest difference.

On the flip side of that, success can be difficult even after you have achieved it, if you are not totally fulfilled. It can be a letdown at times. You end up doubting your success instead of celebrating it, thinking, "Maybe I am not successful yet." Twenty years ago when I opened The Pit, I never thought that it would be this successful. Chuck Liddell, a UFC World Champion, trained here, and his fame has sort of trickled down to us. The Pit is starting to hit the magazines—even Sports Illustrated—and is becoming known for its tough workout. Now I sit back and think, "What's next?" I come up with a whole other list of things I want to achieve. Even after I have reached my financial goals, or my goals as a martial artist, I am still looking for a new goal.

Success has changed my life by giving me comfort and making me secure. It has changed my career by rewarding me with more power to do the things I want within my field. At the MAIA convention in Las Vegas, we couldn't walk ten feet without getting stopped for an autograph, and a picture. Although I know I was a big fish in a small pond, it felt good to be recognized. However, I don't want to just rest on what I've achieved. Because of my success, I set my goals high and expect more out of myself, knowing that I have succeeded in the past.

SOLOMON'S WISDOM:
Success is a gradual process. Even when it's reached, you are not totally fulfilled. Always be thinking, what's next?

CREATING A WONDERFUL LIFE

Michael McCreery

My and my wife's favorite movie is *It's a Wonderful Life*. The movie features Jimmy Stewart and Donna Reed, two staples of wholesome pureness in Hollywood during the 1950s. If you are not familiar with the story, it revolves around George Bailey, played by Stewart, who has dreams of traveling the world and experiencing all that life has to offer. Every time George sets out to live his dream, responsibility for family, friends, and community steps in. Throughout his life, George constantly finds himself having to step up to the plate and do what is right, regardless of how it affects him and his dreams. He does this without complaint. From saving his drowning kid brother to running the family business after his father dies, George takes responsibility because of his obligation to his family, friends, and community.

George finally hits his breaking point when Uncle Billy misplaces a large bank deposit, which will ruin the family business and send Uncle Billy to jail. Our hero will not let that happen to Uncle Billy and steps up yet again to take the responsibility; however, it is not without a price. Our hero loses faith and decides to end it all, because, after all, what good was his life anyway.

An angel named Clarence steps in to give George a glimpse of what life would have been like had he never been born. George realizes that he has made a noticeable difference in the world and returns to face what will surely be a prison sentence for the missing money. However, he now has luck on his side: all of the people he has helped through the years now come forward with money to help him. The refrain is, "If George Bailey needs help, I am there," and the day is saved.

Sappy and sugary sweet, yes, but it still gives me goose bumps as I retell the story. This was just a Hollywood story to me until I started to train in the martial arts. It was then that I discovered that other people not only still believe in sappy Hollywood endings, but they also want to be a part of a family that believes in it too. I tell you this story because to me, the characteristics demonstrated by George represent true success, and I also found these at Action Karate.

Indulge me for a moment as I introduce myself before explaining. My name is Michael McCreery. I am in my early forties, and I married my childhood sweetheart, Linda, twenty-two years ago. We have two wonderful children. Our daughter is a freshman in college, and our son is a sophomore in high school. Prior to training in karate, I represented manufacturers of medical equipment for fifteen years. I started out as a sales representative and worked my way up to a district sales manager. We had a nice house and a vacation every year. However, I had come to hate what I was doing. When I first started, before the proliferation of HMOs, I saw that I was improving the quality of people's lives by helping them manage their pain, for it was a time when the doctor decided what the patient needed. As that changed, I found myself telling people that I could not help them when I knew I could; I became disenfranchised with the industry, and my attitude in general was poor.

This all changed when we signed our three-year-old son up for martial arts lessons at Action Karate. Every week I would observe his instructors painstakingly employ amazing teaching techniques so that his experience was always a positive one, which was not easy. Teaching three year olds karate is a lot like herding cats; even if you can get them together, you need a lot of peroxide and bandages. However, the instructors made it look easy and fun. Intrigued, Linda and I decided to try the adult program and found it every bit as rewarding as the children's program.

A short time later, I offered to help out in my child's class. I discovered that I could teach, was good at it, and could make a difference to a child. From that point, I decided that I was going to open a karate school and help people make themselves stronger physically and mentally. I was like a runaway train, hurrying from my medical business to the karate school every available minute so that I could learn everything I needed to know to be the best instructor I could be. Exactly one week before I received my black belt, Linda and I opened our first school.

I have been married to a beautiful and caring woman for twenty-two years, we have two wonderful children and an active social life with an abundance of great friends, and I love my job! I tell you this not to impress you, but rather to impress upon you that you, too, can create a wonderful life. In this chapter I will give you the strategies that worked for me and that I believe will work for you, too. So without further ado, here are the strategies George employed and I copied to be successful: attitude, responsibility, obligation, community, and fairness.

The Value of Attitude

Attitude: *a settled way of thinking or feeling about someone or something, typically one that is reflected in a person's behavior.*

This is the definition of attitude, straight from the dictionary. While it makes sense, I think it lacks one important element: choice. Whether we realize it or not, we all make a choice every day about our attitude. Regardless of what happened to him, George chose to keep his best foot forward.

"The truth is that a positive thought always overcomes a negative one. This is the natural law. When the sun rises, the fog vanishes. When the light is switched on, the darkness disappears." (Unknown)

I believe with all my heart that any success I enjoy in life always goes back to my attitude. No matter what happens to me, I am blessed with the ability to make a choice every day and focus on the positive. I believe that this was instilled in me early on by my parents. My parents are amazing, for they somehow managed to guide four boys to adulthood and care for my severely handicapped older sister. Developmentally, my sister is the equivalent of a four-year-old. Not once in my formative years did I hear, "Why me?" or "It is not fair." My sister was my sister, and our parents realized that it was what it was. No whining, no complaining—it was life: deal with it. While both of my parents had a huge influence on me, looking back, it was my mother who always had the positive outlook that I now possess.

In my job I have had the opportunity to work with a great many people over long periods of time. Time and time again I have seen examples of how attitude can tear you down or build you up to success. I know a woman who is constantly asking, "Why don't people like me? I do not get it. I am a good person"; however; if you walk into a room full of people, there she would sit with her body turned away from the crowd and her nose in the air as though she were smelling the worst thing in the world. She puts out an attitude of inapproachability. The scary part to me is people's inability to realize that they are choosing a negative attitude every day when they wake up. That attitude jades and colors every experience they have. The reverse works as well; people who choose to keep a positive attitude find themselves looking at challenges from a much different viewpoint. Their outlook tends to put them in problem-solving mode. It is just the opposite for their negative counterparts: they seem to fall into the "why me" mindset and become the captain of their sinking ship.

Step number one to creating your wonderful life is to realize that attitude is an outward expression of an inward feeling, and when anything rots, it is usually from the inside out. With few exceptions, you decide how you feel inside. If this is a challenge for you, then try turning around negative thoughts as soon as they enter your mind, using a process called reformatting.

When you feel angry, think love.
If you face dishonesty, think integrity.
If there is miserliness, think generosity.
If there is jealousy, think nobility.
If there is timidity, think courage.

The Value of Responsibility

Responsibility: *the state or fact of having a duty to deal with something or of having control over someone.*

George was all about responsibility. It was a core value for him. He did the responsible thing no matter what the personal consequences may have been. To me, personal responsibility may be the lynchpin to all success. There I was, working in a job that I hated for years, doing the same thing over and over. There was no winning lottery ticket to solve all my problems. If I wanted things to change, I had to change them, and signing our son up for karate showed me the way.

I was at least two and a half years away from being able to test for my black belt. I knew enough to be dangerous but not enough to open and run a school. I had the work ethic and the passion, but not the knowledge, so I took responsibility. I wrote up a plan that would take me up to black belt testing and get me the knowledge I would need to accomplish my goal. If it was to be, it was up to me. I had developed a passion for teaching and making a difference in people's lives, just as my instructors, Solomon Brenner and Jacqueline Razzi had made a difference to my family and me.

If you are reading this book because you have a goal to be more successful in your life, please remember that a goal in your head is just a wish, not a goal. To be successful, you must commit to paper what it is that you want; that makes it a goal. When I decided to open a martial arts school as an orange belt, just nine months into my training, I knew that I needed a plan. I wrote out everything from the appearance of the school to the *It's a Wonderful Life* philosophy. I created an image for myself, a picture that was so motivating that I found a way to make it happen. Quick! Go get a pencil and paper. The time has come to take responsibility for your new life.

Step number two to creating your wonderful life is to figure out what it is that you really want. What is your ideal job? What would your ideal relationship look like? What is it that you are passionate about? Take your time and write it all down. Are you done? Now how can you take responsibility to make it happen? That is an important question, because my experience with people is that a lot of them will write up a list of all the things that their spouse, children, or employer have to change. Hello! You are missing the point; *you* need to take responsibility. It is about *you*—no one else. How are you going to solve the problem? Once you have the basic outline for what it is that you want and how you are going to take responsibility for it, write yourself a story that gets you there. Include as much detail as possible, everything from the color of the walls to what it smells like. It sounds silly, but I believe my ability to succeed is directly linked to how compelling of a picture I paint for myself.

The Value of Obligation

Obligation: *an act or course of action to which a person is morally or legally bound; a duty or commitment.*

George never met an obligation to which he did not rise. If responsibility is the lynchpin to success, then obligation is the piece held in place by the lynchpin. I believe that responsibility and obligation are like success and celebration; you cannot have one without the other.

On October 12, 1987, one of the most important events in my life occurred. My beautiful wife gave birth to our first child, Danielle. I was there for the whole thing, and when I saw my daughter, I immediately started to cry uncontrollably. It was the purest joy and love I have ever felt. Before I went out to tell my in-laws, who were in the waiting room, I had to compose myself. I was afraid that if they saw me crying when I came out, they would think the worst before I could say a word. I made it to "It's a ..." before once again the waterworks started. I composed myself again and called my parents. This time it was, "It's a girl!" and I lost it again.

I tell you this story, because I believe most people can understand the obligation of parent to child. The sacrifices that a parent makes for a child are amazing: sleep deprivation, sitting by the side of a toilet rubbing their back as they expel unmentionable things, doing what is right even when our reward is, "I hate you," a lifetime of debt for their education, even when they move back home after they graduate because they still have not found themselves. Yet we do it all in the name of love and obligation. Just imagine for a moment how great this world would be if we viewed all obligations with that kind of commitment.

Call me silly, but I believe marriage is till death do you part. Relax; sit down. I know there are exceptions to every rule, like addiction and infidelity, just to name a few; however, I believe that we spend too much time trying to figure out how to get out of things and not enough time trying to fix them ourselves. I am obligated to do everything in my power to make my marriage work. I do not focus on how to get out of it. I focus on how to make it great. I am obligated to equip my children with the necessary skills to never need me again. I am obligated to run my business in a responsible manner for the sake of my employees and customers.

Step number three to creating your wonderful life: embrace obligation.

The Value of Community

Community: *a group of people living together in one place.*

A big part of George's commitment was to try to provide affordable housing to working-class families, because the local bank would not. I believe community is what solidifies your family, group, or business in this world.

My fifteen-year-old son, Michael, got this whole karate thing rolling when we signed him up at the age of three. In twelve years Michael has never said to me, "Dad, I do not want to go to karate today." As a matter of fact, he makes me pick him up every day after school and bring him there, not because he is required to, but rather, because he wants to be there. He is a paid part-time instructor and a co-captain of our performance team, a team that performs karate at events ranging from elementary school picnics to the halftime show for the Philadelphia 76ers. He constantly amazes me with his ability to interact and perform at a level of maturity that is well past his biological years.

The other day I was teaching class and I observed Michael walking through the front door of the school. As he made his way through the parent area, he was stopped no less than eight times by parents asking how their children were doing in class, or commenting on a recent performance he had done, or just socializing with him as they would any other adult—except this adult is fifteen. It occurred to me that the sense of community that this child has grown up in has empowered him with a connection and maturity well beyond his years.

That takes me to the next step in success: creating a community/family. In my world, these two words are interchangeable. Whether you are working on your family, church, business, or martial arts school, you need to create a sense of community. Here are the steps that we used to create a rock solid community: create an empowering environment that provides lots of positive feedback in public and provides correction in private. Praise makes you stand up straight and beam, public correction humiliates you and makes you shrink. Empower people with the ability to be more than just a student. Give them more than what they expect. We do not teach karate; we teach people. We use karate as a vehicle to empower them. Every lesson includes a mental benefit and ways to apply it at home, school, and work. We provide performance teams and leadership teams for students to further empower them.

In short, step number four is creating a place to which people can belong. It is a powerful need: the need to belong to something bigger than just themselves.

The Value of Fairness

Fairness: *free from bias, dishonesty, or injustice; legitimately sought, pursued, done, given, etcetera.*

George's fairness to all of the people he dealt with was evident in everything he did. Fairness is what makes the community embrace you as an individual, family, or business. Ricky was a mischievous, fun-loving, challenging child when he began at our school at the age of five. Though challenging, he was the kind of a child in whose eyes you could see a spark that said, "I will be something someday." The biggest challenge with this type of child is teaching him control and self-discipline without breaking his spirit. Over the years, he matured and grew as he went through the belt ranks. Still mischievous, but definitely more mature, he became eligible for black belt testing. Although concerned that he was not applying himself at the necessary level to accomplish the goal, I gave him the opportunity, nonetheless.

The day of the test arrived. As Ricky worked hard physically, it made me proud to see him push in the long workout. During the self-defense test he struggled a little bit, but not too bad. When it came time to perform his katas, it all fell apart. He had not dedicated the time necessary to accomplish the required level of proficiency. I felt bad for him, but he knew the requirements. One of the most important parts of fairness is setting clearly defined rules. "When can I earn my next belt, Mr. McCreery?" "When I think you are ready," would be the reply at a lot of schools. At Action Karate the reply would be, "The minimum standard to earn your next belt is twenty-one to twenty-four classes, and you must perform your kata in class with no assistance from an instructor; then you will be eligible for your next belt." "When can I test for my black belt, Mr. McCreery?" "The minimum standard to test for your black belt is three years of committed training."

I asked Ricky after his test whether he felt that he had done everything he could to be prepared for the test. "No, Mr. McCreery. I was not prepared the way I should have been, and I have failed. Nothing could be worse than that." I then explained to Ricky that this was just another step in his journey, and that there are a lot worse things than failing, such as accepting a belt that you did not really earn. Ricky agreed, and six months later he did the necessary work and passed his black belt test.

I believe that I am living a wonderful life; I look forward to every day with excitement, whether it is going to work or staying at home. A silly Hollywood movie has become the foundation for creating success for me and my family. I really believe that anyone can create a wonderful life as well, if they remember the values of a wonderful life.

Attitude is yours to choose every day, good or bad.

Responsibility is the cornerstone for maturity.

Obligations and living up to them shows people that you are dependable.

Community gives the power of numbers; it is easier to raise a child with a village than it is to do it alone.

Fairness and good common sense should always be the basis for decision-making.

I was thirty-two years old before I laid out the plan to create my wonderful life, and it all happened because I took the time to write out my dream. Stop waiting and start writing your wonderful life.

S O L O M O N ' S   W I S D O M :
*Anyone can choose success. The first step is to choose
a positive attitude and then create a plan for
your wonderful life!*

Michael McCreery has been married to his wife Linda for twenty-five years. He and his wife started training in the Martial Arts in 1995, and they received their black belts in 1998. The opened Action Karate in New Britain, Pennsylvania, the week before they earned their black belts. They have a twenty-two-year-old daughter, Danielle and a nineteen-year-old son, Michael Jr.

Both are black belts. Mr. McCreery specializes in character development and in helping children and adults raise their level of achievement. He is available for motivational, child safety, and self-protection seminars. Mr. McCreery can be reached at 215-348-7110 or actionkarate@verizon.net.

MY SECRETS TO SUCCESS

Melody Shuman

With a bio that would make any parent proud on paper, I have found that most of my successful secrets have come from mounds of mistakes. Unfortunately, I have made so many mistakes that if someone asked me if I wanted to start over in life I would jump at the offer. Fortunately, I took notes along the way that just may change the life of another. If so, then I have served my purpose in life and perhaps would reconsider my statement.

Saying that brings me to my primary objective within this chapter. That primary objective is to provide you with secrets that have lead me to success, along with a clear explanation of how to make these secrets work for you. As I say in all of my consulting reports: Let's get started!

Secret 1: I became an expert at something.

Experts are respected because—well—they are experts! If you have the knowledge, the power and drive to master something, and the ability to translate your skills in an easy-to-follow format, then dub yourself an expert. If not, then get to work! The main ingredient in a successful recipe is expertise. Without it, you are not a success but a mere copycat or imitation of the real thing.

I ran an extremely successful martial arts school that boasted thirty-six world-champion titles. The problem was that we were turning over more under-qualified students than talented ones. It hit me one day after I had judged a testing of five- and six-year olds that had demonstrated absolutely no improvement from the previous testing. I actually think they got worse within eight weeks! It was at that moment that I realized I either was going to be an expert at teaching children, or I was going to find something more rewarding and productive. My own demise set up my biggest success story.

I started with my worst class: six and under children. Until then, I had been teaching these kids a watered-down version of our regular curriculum. Let me say that again: "I was teaching a *watered-down* version of our regular curriculum." I was actually telling parents of our six and under kids that their program was *watered-down*. Why do I keep emphasizing the words *watered-down*? Because to this day I still cannot believe that I thought a *watered-down* version of a curriculum that was originally developed for adult men was appropriate for kids that young.

Our six and under kids were kicking the same way for every type of kick that I taught them. Their front kicks, side kicks, and round kicks looked exactly alike. I tried to correct them, but it didn't make much of a difference.

This taught me that kids this age obviously did not have the physical strength in their legs to adjust the motion of each kick. This led me to the conclusion that their balance was poor. This led me to the conclusion that their control was not very good. This led me to the conclusion that their main muscle groups still needed time to develop. This made me recognize that I was only beginning to discover how my *watered-down* program was nowhere near as beneficial to children as I thought it was.

Discovering that I had a lot to learn helped me discover that we all had a lot to learn as martial arts instructors when it comes to teaching children. With that said, the Little Ninja program was born. I dedicated myself to learning as much as I could about kids six and under. I became an expert at children's martial arts education and started on my path to success by becoming the best at what I did.

The Little Ninja program is the most popular children's martial arts program in the world. Over 2,500 schools in over nine countries use this innovative program. I spent three years traveling around the world on behalf of the National Association of Professional Martial Artists (NAPMA). After the creation of the Little Ninja program, I continued my studies to create four more age-specific martial arts programs. The Future Kidz Series (ages three to four and five to six) and the Karate Kidz Zone series (ages seven to nine and ten to fourteen) have helped hundreds of martial arts schools take their business to a new generation of children's education.

Becoming an expert at children's martial arts education lead to my most prized possession: an award from living martial arts legend, Chuck Norris. Mr. Norris presented me with a plaque at his annual United Fighting Arts Federation (UFAF) event in front of over one thousand spectators. This award was a huge milestone in my career, and has motivated me to continue my drive to be the best at what I do.

My success secret number 1: Find something that you not only love, but are pretty good at and then become the best at it. If you are not fully committed to becoming not just great at what you do, but the *expert* at what you do, then read no further, because you are missing the most important ingredient that cannot be replaced in your recipe for success.

Secret 2: I set a value for myself.

Let me take you on a journey to your own self-destruction.

The worst thing that you can do in your career is be very good at something and then not charge what you deserve for your contributions. The second worst thing you can do for your career is to work very hard—all of the time—and not have any free time to enjoy life. The third worst thing you can do for your career is to work very hard, knowing that you should earn more, and still keep going down that same self-destructive path.

Success equals a tipped scale of income versus effort. You are successful if you get paid what you deserve for what you do. You are not successful if you work harder than what you get paid for. If you make a million dollars but work a million hours, then you are not successful. If you make a million dollars but have more leisure time during the week than work time, then you are successful. Success is more than just a dollar sign—it is a dollar symbol.

My success secret number 2: Rate yourself into a higher equation of success than what you are comfortable with, and then make sure that you are worth it.

Secret 3: I am working on mastering my leadership skills.

Got something you think will take you to the top? Make sure that you have enough people behind you that can help take you there. If not, then you are going to experience a slow and painful reality check of how success really works. You *must* be a leader of your vision. You must be able to translate that vision to others in a manner that intrinsically motivates them to help you accomplish that vision.

You can pay a person to work for you. The problem is, if they are not moved by your vision, your ideas, or your goals for your team's future, then you are going to consistently hit a wall of obstacles that will limit your success. To be successful, you must have a team of individuals who are not guided by titles or incentives, but by pure leadership that places people in positions that stand for more.

A good leader understands the difference between extrinsic (external) stimulation versus intrinsic (internal) stimulation. A leader identifies the real meaning behind a team. A leader can take an individual or a group of one hundred people in a direction of meaning and purpose without having to rely on bribes, incentives, or special recognition. True leadership stems from a person that who doesn't have to ask for assistance or take all of the credit. The most successful people are the first to turn to their team and say that it happened because of their unselfish contributions.

My success secret number 3: If you have enough people who admire you and will follow your guidance because they believe in your vision, then you have the necessary leadership skills that will help make dreams come true.

Secret 4: I learned to maximize my creativity during the least expected hours of the day.

It's a funny thought, but when I list the times during which I come up with some of my greatest ideas, it is not during work hours, but at times when you would least expect it—such as when I take a shower, watch football, lie on the beach, listen to live music, and the list goes on. Did you notice that all of the creative moments in my life are during leisure hours? It reminds me about why vacations and activities that provide meditation time are so important.

Think about it.

How much wasted time do we consume when we are sitting at our workspace tapping our pencils, wracking our brains, and flipping through countless resources only to find ourselves no closer to success than when we woke up that day? Fortunately, there is a secret that you would least expect, but many successful people recognize that it brings them closer to success each and every moment: the moments when they are away from their workspace!

It is no wonder why we see bosses, CEOs, and entrepreneurs take more vacations than ever, yet still manage to run some of the most successful companies on the planet. Their secret is balance. They understand the psychological science of how a healthy balance between life and work generates more success than a day consumed with more work and less play.

Successful people have discovered that they generate more creative juices when they are enjoying life the most; hence the motivation to continue with success. They relax their mind, body, and soul. When they find themselves in a relaxed-calm state of mind, they recognize that it makes them feel so good that their minds begin to euphorically generate more and more creative ideas that will put them into even more relaxing experiences like their current ones.

My success secret number 4: Spend time enjoying life, and you'll find yourself building creative juices that lead to success.

Secret 5: I pamper my dreams.

Have you ever watched someone you truly admire and wonder what it would be like if you were in his or her shoes? Have you ever test-driven a car that you knew you really couldn't afford at the moment, but would like to have one day? Have you ever driven in a neighborhood that was far more expensive than you could afford, yet you told yourself that someday you would have a home like the ones you see?

If so, then you possess the same characteristic that successful people have. It shifts their momentum into full gear. That characteristic is *curiosity*.

I am a very curious person. I ask what I do not know. I seek what I cannot find. I reach for what I cannot touch. Curiosity makes me try. Without curiosity I would not ask questions. Without curiosity I would not read to find answers. Without curiosity I would not set goals that I know will be challenging. I would be in a consistent "comfort state" each and every day. I would never put myself to the test. I would give up often. Without curiosity I would be nothing more than a shadow going through the motions, and no one would recognize me.

Are you a shadow or a ray of light?

To shine through the obstacles and boundaries that lie in front of you, you must first master the secret of curiosity. You must explore areas of interest or desire. You must rise above your own comfort zones to seek possibilities that are beyond your reach. Curiosity stimulates your mind and forces you to take a second look at what you are capable of.

My success secret number 5: Take a drive along a beautiful neighborhood road, read a memoir of someone you admire, and imagine yourself in a bigger, better place than you are today. There is no ingredient that makes a recipe successful like a spoonful of curiosity. Try it—I guarantee that you will like it!

SOLOMON'S WISDOM
The best ideas and creativity sometimes come from down time away from work.

SUCCESS

Melody Shuman holds a Fifth Degree Black Belt in Taekwondo and is the owner and chief instructor of On the Mat Martial Arts. She is also a business and children's Martial Arts consultant. You can reach her via e-mail at: melody@shumanconcepts.com, or check out her Web sites: www.onthematma.com, www.shuman-concepts.com, and www.conceptforkids.com.

A POSITIVE MINDSET

Ed Parker Jr.

Success is relative. One can be successful at waking up in the morning. But one must have a vision of what it means to be successful at something greater in one's life. For me, success is realizing one's goals and visions in life, and then cycling through it again with new and different goals. Success is the bliss of being lost in the work, the joy of the journey, not the destination.

Success starts with meditating and becoming clear about what I wish to attain in my life, then focusing on it so that it becomes like a photograph in my mind. Then I try and make it into a three-dimensional object in my mind, so I can see its height, width, and depth from all angles. The more real it looks in my head, the more I can manifest its reality in my life.

Look at your goal as though it were a memory—a future memory that hasn't happened yet. Who is there? Where are they sitting or standing? What time of day is it? Where are you? What are you wearing? Envision it as clearly as possible, as though it has already happened.

To achieve success, you have to be passionate about what you do or about the vision you have. Find that one thing that excites you and motivates you to wake up early every morning or go to bed late every night, just because you are anxious to work on your tasks for accomplishing your vision.

Stay focused and follow through with the tasks that it takes to achieve your goals. Don't let emotions dictate your goals, but rather let your plan dictate them. You have to care about them; the only way in which you should let your emotions affect your goals is to motivate you.

If you're working on a task, however, take that emotion away. If your goal is large, it is easy to become bored or get discouraged when it doesn't work out. The most important thing to do is to break it off into smaller goals that lay the foundation for the overall goal to be accomplished. I forgive myself for not getting a task done. It's possible that I set the goal too high and need to readjust. You need to readjust every day.

Reaching your goals is like the saying, "How do you eat an elephant?" The answer: "One bite at a time."

People can become frustrated with their goals when they don't set enough small goals. Saying you want $1 million is a big leap. Think about your goal as a sculpture you're building. Start with a good foundation to make any progress.

Words are important to achieving goals and success. I don't like using the following words: *failure, good, bad, right,* or *wrong.* I prefer *effective* or *ineffective.* Some people analyze from a negative point of view. We have a tendency to destroy ourselves by using negative words such as failure. If you start out negatively, you have to fight just to get to neutral ground. But if you start by using neutral words, you work your way up to positive ground.

We are bound to have non-successes, but don't think of them

as failures. Failure is a title, a state of being. We dig ourselves into a negative hole, and it takes a lot of energy just to get out onto neutral ground. It's all in the way we program our minds. To me, failure and success are camp-out places. The joy is in the journey, the work, the progress. We should constantly set new goals, stay busy, and be proactive.

I have "failed" many times, but that is irrelevant, as it is bound to happen to anyone. Just pick yourself up, forgive yourself, and get back to life. The key is to reprogram the mind. The term *failure* is a word that I do not use with my internal dialogue. I replace that with, "Okay, that did not work," or, "Let me try it a different way." People have a tendency to feel badly when things do not work out; then they feel badly for feeling badly. I refer that type of thinking as compounding a negative thought process, which is detrimental toward accomplishing one's dreams and goals. Feeling badly or feeling discouraged is a natural thing, but to compound it with negative words and emotions is fruitless wasted energy.

When you feel as though you are not making any progress with your goal, as if you have hit a wall and success has escaped you, take a step back. Your view of the situation is based solely on your perspective. I blend art and martial arts, and at times I juggle fifteen pieces of art at once. In my art training, sometimes I'd be working on a piece that just wasn't coming out the way I'd imagined it. I'd put more and more work into it, but sometimes it still wouldn't manifest. I had to learn how to let it go for a while, work on something else, and then come back to it with fresh eyes. This is what it sometimes takes to accomplish a goal—fresh perspective. Don't be afraid to let go. Don't abandon your goal, but give yourself a break.

Don't allow distractions and interruptions to influence your goals. Distractions are inevitable but must be regarded as irrelevant to your overall goal. In other words, do not place much emotion into those distractions or setbacks. Emotions can slow down the process tremendously.

When you let someone else influence your emotions, you decide how much energy to give them versus how much you give yourself. Most opinions are negative, and we buy into that negativity. We actually sometimes have a fear of succeeding when we don't know what will come after success.

I once met a woman who worked in sales and then went on to get a degree in social work. When her new career path didn't work out, she felt like a failure. But why? She accomplished her goal, it just wasn't fulfilling to her. It wasn't where she was meant to be.

You are in control of your own success. You need a clear vision of the variables that could affect your goals and a clear vision of how you will deal with them. You decide how much brainpower you want to invest in negative or positive thinking and how much you want to let someone else influence you. You can let someone influence your thoughts without letting them dominate your goals.

I use what I call the collective mind. The arrogant man believes that all things are found within his mind. He hits obstacles because he is not able to ask others for help, advice, or answers. Using the collective minds of those surrounding you is what provides an unlimited supply of knowledge and ideas. Just harvest the people in your life with the talent they have to assist in your overall goal. I do believe that you are the people with whom you surround yourself. So it is important to have a friendship base and a social circle with those who provide a good harvest.

My dad was one of the most influential martial artists on the planet. He could teach an idea or concept without terminology. People always thought he had all the answers. What would really happen was that he would throw out ideas; he'd act as though he were quizzing the students, when really they were giving him the answers. If he didn't know the terminology for something, he would ask, and someone else would give him the answer. It's using the collective mind. When you can use the minds of others who have knowledge that you don't have, you can seek perspective and use it for the greater good.

I believe in the art of self-defense against one's self. We will beat ourselves up more than anyone else ever would, so we must practice restraint on self-sabotage. Minimize negative thoughts. I usually find that when people offer me a compliment about how they feel about what I do, that I must not ruin the moment with my opinion, if my opinion opposes what was said to me. That goes in the reverse as well.

I don't use negative words to describe myself. I don't beat myself up. We are our own greatest obstacles. We need to reprogram the way we define ourselves. People tend to perpetuate negativity. For example, one guy will begin a story: "Oh, man, the car dealer really ripped me off today ..." Then someone else will inevitably reply with, "That's nothing! Wait until you hear what happened to *me* ..." It's about choosing to look at the glass as half full rather than half empty. Spend time generating something positive rather than regurgitating the negative.

Think about the soil. California is one big desert, yet in Pasadena, where I live, there are beautiful trees everywhere. That's because people have nurtured the soil and made things grow. In the same way, we have to nurture our lives, our souls, so that something good can come out of us as well.

Here's another analogy. In art college, I learned that all color, form, and shape are defined by how light is reflected. Thus, the sun defines life. The sun gives us everything that our eyes can feast on, asking nothing in return. Rather than constantly giving like the sun, a black hole is constantly taking. It destroys all color, form, and shape, is always hungry for more, and is never satisfied. If you are constantly giving, you generate your own source of positive energy from which you and those around you can benefit.

I was born into the martial arts industry; I didn't choose it. I don't know any other life. I was greatly influenced by my father, Ed Parker, Sr., and his understanding of martial arts. He grew up in Hawaii and was taught traditional martial arts, but he took a smart, logical approach. One idea with which my dad experimented was that of the opposite and reverse. He would watch a film of himself doing a form, and then watch it in reverse, seeing it from a new perspective.

For example, what would you do if someone told you to do the opposite of a right horizontal thrust punch? The first thing that comes to mind may be a left horizontal thrust punch, but that's not really the opposite. You have to look at all the variables. Don't limit your mind. Break it down word by word. The opposite of right is, obviously, left. What is the opposite of horizontal? Well, that could be vertical or diagonal. What is the opposite of thrust? You could do nothing, or you could snap a punch or kick. What's the opposite of a punch? Anything that's not a punch: a kick, a chop, etcetera.

You see, by looking at all of the variables you can expand your mind. Sometimes people spend too much energy trying to be right, and they don't think about being effective. Stop the drama cycle; don't think about right and wrong. Think about how you can become more effective. Take martial arts, for example. In a confrontation, a martial artist would most likely have the skills to defend himself if necessary. But the point of martial arts is to get to a point where you don't need to use martial arts.

In his early life, my father's idea of martial arts focused more on the physical, but as he got older, he started to focus on the spiritual. One time a group of people came into my father's school to pick a fight with him for some reason or other. My father said, "Okay," then turned around and started rummaging through his desk drawers. He pulled out a pencil. The men look slightly confused. Then my father pulls out a sheet of paper. One of the men asked what he was doing. "Hold on," he said. "I have to sharpen my pencil." He proceeds to calmly sharpen his pencil. Losing patience, one guy said, "We're going to kick your ass!" My father said, "Fine; but first I'll need you to write down your names and when you'd like to die." The men just stood there looking at him. My father explained, "Your options are to die before you hit the floor, to die in the hospital of complications in a few hours, or to die of complications in a few months. I need your names so that I can tell the cops what to put in the police report." The men left and my father never had to lift a finger. He became so secure in his physical abilities that he didn't even have to use them.

The same concept can be applied to reaching your goals. When an obstacle presents itself, look at all of the variables and use your mind to examine the problem before you even lift a finger. Sam Brown was an axe fighter who lived around the time of Abraham Lincoln. He was only 5'4", but he wanted desperately to fight the 6'5" Lincoln. He was always looking for an opportunity to fight him. Finally, he told Abe to name any time and place for them to fight. Abe said, "Time: 6:00 tomorrow morning. Place: 5'5" of water." Sam Brown thanked Lincoln for sparing his life and teaching him a lesson. Learn to use your mind to fight. It can often be your most powerful weapon.

Success shouldn't be a place where you camp out. As soon as you reach a goal, start working toward a new one. Also take time to reflect back at pivotal points of your life to check things off your to-do list. I use a personal philosophy that I call an "ego bank account." To spend your successes with arrogance is a misuse of that power. Power is best used when no one is around. When life gets tough for me, sometimes I go in my back yard and lie in my hammock and make a withdrawal from my ego back account. Never spend your ego moment at the time it is earned. Place those moments in your ego savings for another time.

I continue to grow by living, not just existing. Be proactive in all that you do. Give of yourself every day. Help others in their paths. Meditate and envision your future and what it looks like. Stop and live in the moment. Look at nature every day. Love your family and friends. Teach others. Be nice to others. Be honest.

Books I recommend:

- *Infinite Insights into Kenpo*, volumes 1–5, by Ed Parker Sr.
- *The Zen of Kenpo*, by Ed Parker Sr.
- *Absorb What Is Useful*, by Dan Inasanto
- *Zen in the Martial Arts*, by Joe Hyamns.
- *The Tao of Jeet Kun Do*, by Bruce Lee

SOLOMON'S WISDOM:
Remember to stay positive and give to others. Be like the sun, not like the black hole.

Edmund Kealoha Parker, Jr. (professionally known as Ed Parker, Jr.) was born in Glendale, California to the late Ed Parker, Sr., Senior Grandmaster and founder of American Kenpo karate. Ed, in his own right, has become an accomplished martial artist. He has:

- *Co-published and designed over twenty martial arts books*
- *Produced six educational martial arts videos*
- *Published The Encyclopedia of Kenpo, a complete reference resource on American Kenpo karate*
- *Ed has appeared or worked with Chuck Norris, James Colburn, Kareem Abdul Jabbar, Wesley Snipes, Steven Ho, Don "the dragon" Wilson, Jeff Speakman and Benny "The Jet" Urquidez.*
- *He hosted "The Night of the Golden Masters," a martial arts special scheduled for Showtime*
- *He completed the fight choreography for the movie Deadly*

Takeover (starring, Jeff Speakman and veteran actor, Ron Silver)

- *In the year 2004, he founded EPAKS, Inc. a company dedicated toward the publishing and producing of high quality teaching and learning materials for the martial arts industry.*
- *Appeared in a major Hollywood film by Universal Studios called Dragon, the Bruce Lee Story.*
- *During the past twenty years Ed has taught martial arts seminars in fourteen countries and over forty states. To date he has taught over 30,000 people.*

Ed has worked for over thirty years as a freelance illustrator and graphic artist. He worked on numerous design campaigns and has produced over 10,000 pieces of artwork, a series of portraits of prominent individuals within martial arts and the Kenpo industry. Thus far, over 800 portraits have been completed. He has designed a line of clothing and a martial arts uniform and is the current owner of a custom-illustrated award company for the Martial Arts industry.

Ed is the proud father of four children—three daughters: Jessica, Joanna, Jayde and one son, Edmund Parker III; he is also the Grandfather of three. He lives with his wife Silvia in Pasadena, California.

Contact information:

For custom-illustrated rank certificates and awards as well as custom hand-illustrated portraits.

Artnative Creative Group, Inc.
Ed Parker, Jr. Diplomas
2245 East Colorado Blvd. #104 PMB 257
Pasadena, CA 91107
Call toll free:
1-866-919-5425

ALL IN THE FAMILY

Ernie Reyes

To me, success is finding out what you love doing most and being able to make it your passion, your art, your profession, and your life! I believe that I am blessed to have found what I love doing most, my noble calling in life: becoming a masterful martial artist and martial arts teacher.

Success is to conquer yourself during your lifetime. The logo of our West Coast World Martial Arts is composed of a circular three-bladed martial arts edge. The bottom blade represents you, the individual; the second blade moving clockwise represents the students; and the third blade represents our association, friends, and family. The ideal scene of success would be to have all three parts of the blade become successful, but in order for that to happen, you must become successful first and foremost. Then and only then can you bring success to the other blades. So sharpen your blade first! Each and every day and in every way getting greater, greater, and greater!

My success was made possible through having the opportunity to learn from great martial arts old school teachers, Grand Masters Dan Choi and Mosises Arizmendi, who taught me the highest values of martial arts training: honor, loyalty, family, and bravery, built upon the foundation of respect and discipline. I have never forgotten these basic—but very powerful—principles that have been the roots of my success and accomplishments during my forty-four years of martial arts training and teaching.

The people with whom you surround yourself on a daily basis are bringing you either happiness or sadness, positive or negative energy. To me, team is everything. Our executive team of masters—Tony Thompson, Margie Betke, Donna Bernardi, Smitesh Parmar, our West Coast World Martial Arts school owners, and myself—have been role models of black belt loyalty and dedication to success for decades. Success for yourself is good, but success for your entire team is great. I have never ever thought about becoming successful just for myself; it has always been for the greater good of our teams, whether our martial arts teams, my martial arts school team or my professional business teams.

To become successful quickly, effectively, and efficiently, it takes a team of people who all have the same beliefs, values, and vision. If you want success, team up with successful people; if you want failure, team up with people who are failing. If you can transform your team into a family, this is the highest level of team. Now, not only are people working together because of a worthwhile cause, they are now also giving their hearts and souls to their work to achieve success. Choose your teams wisely!

Our West Coast World Martial Arts Association leaders have not only developed great teams, but we have also built a great family culture. My greatest passion is still the love of teaching. My training partner of over forty years, Tony Thompson, and I have built an association of affliated martial arts schools across the United States; this is a martial arts success that I cherish. It is one of our greatest successes to have impacted and empowered hundreds of thoundsands of students' and people's lives through our West Coast World Martial Arts Black Belt and Mastery Success and training teaching system:

1. Black belt is the goal
2. Start training consistently, *now*
3. Strive for black belt excellence
4. Practice, practice, perfectly
5. Create mastery or success

Set a goal and create a powerful driven purpose that is integrated into your heart and soul so that you never, ever think about quitting for any reason until you accomplish your goal or success. My goal and driven purpose is one word: mastery. I am committed to strive for mastery every day of my life!

You have to develop a black belt mindset. Without a powerful black belt mindset of believing in yourself and your ability to give 110 percent in everything you do, your goals of succeeding will only be dreams. A black belt mindset teaches you to develop the mindsct of no retreat, no surrender until your mission is accomplished. Black belt mindset means achieving a high level of excellence or mastery in martial arts and life. It means not only becoming a black belt in martial arts but also becoming a black belt in life and learning to give unconditional love and respect to yourself and others.

You are the only person who can stand in the way of your success. Your belief in personal limits, fear of the unknown, fear of rejection, lack of work ethic, lack of constant commitment, not taking massive action and not having a strong enough driven purpose are the major opponents that you will have to fight and conquer. These roadblocks will stand in your way to success. You must have a strong driven purpose that you believe in each and every day to win these battles of adversity.

When I was a child in grammar school, I had trouble reading, writing, spelling, and understanding math. As a matter of fact, I failed the first grade and was held back. I was afraid to go school because I had trouble learning and because I just couldn't understand or comprehend academic issues. All I wanted to do was play sports, something I excelled in. The challenge of learning was a big setback for me emotionally until around eighth and ninth grade when I made up my mind that I no longer wanted to be thought of as a person that was looked upon as dumb. This was a compelling moment in my life to learn to overcome obstacles.

I made a commitment to myself that I was going to transform my learning process and give extraordinary effort to studying to raise my grade point average. I used this handicap as motivation! I thought about why I was excelling in sports. Because I was putting massive amounts of time into learning athletics, I was achieving all-league honors. Now it was time for me to do the same in my academics. I surrounded myself with friends who were honor students and others like me that wanted to make a difference. We had to study much longer and put in more time just to catch up. In high school, I made the honor roll and I eventually graduated from San Jose State University with a degree in Business Administration.

As you get older you realize that life isn't going to be perfect. You can use failure as a positive learning process. Everyone has goals and dreams that sometimes are not going to be possible for whatever reason. The most important thing is that you learn to give 110 percent to whatever desired goal you want to accomplish, because you will always learn something of value to improve your mindset or yourself personally if you look for it.

Trying to stay positive is challenging when things don't seem to formulate. These are valuable and powerful moments that can strengthen you if you realize that this is a life lesson that can be thought of as only a setback and not the end of a new beginning. Use failure as motivation! You don't need to change your goal, but sometimes you just need to make a slight change in your strategy of how you are going about accomplishing it. If you change your approach, sometimes a failure can become a success.

In 1977, I fought in the third Tae Kwon Do World Championships in Chicago. I was fighting the Korean national champion. I was over trained up to the day of the competition, and a few days before the tournament I was spitting blood from getting hit in the throat. I had bronchitis, and no doubt the Korean champion had more international experience and reputation than I had at the time. Because of my martial arts training, I still gave my heart and soul to never quit! I eventually won the bronze medal and was grateful to have experienced the journey of what it takes to become a champion. I failed in getting the gold but, just as when I had failed in getting a basketball scholarship in Junior College because of a foot injury, it gave me the opportunity to do what I love doing most, and that is becoming a dedicated martial arts teacher.

I had the opportunity to become successful in producing seven National Forms champions in one year from my school, one of which, my son Ernie Reyes, Jr. was the youngest child to ever be rated in a professional martial arts adults division at eight years old. I had the opportunity to become successful in teaching one of the best martial arts demonstration teams in the world and travel the globe with them. It was called the West Coast Demonstration Team, eventually called the Ernie Reyes' World Action Team. These unexpected earlier failures brought me success in what I love doing most: teaching others.

To succeed, you must never lose passion. Never take it for granted; it is like becoming a world champion. The great ones are not satisfied in just winning a world champion belt for the day. They have developed a black belt mindset for how they are going to defend it. The ones that are remembered are the ones who hold on to their title year after year. I have seen martial artists who have succeeded in the past take it for granted that the hard work and dedication it took them to get there is not necessary anymore to succeed. They lose their passion to teach; they think just about the money and then they get burnt out. Martial arts is pure and ethical. If you don't respect the art, the art will not allow you to succeed. It's all about the constant and consistent commitment to keep on learning, training, and succeeding forever!

In the early 1980s I had developed seven National Forms champions who revolutionized musical creative forms in the United States, and we had one of the most famous martial arts demonstration teams in the world. I thought that we had something special, and we wanted to impact the world on a bigger scale with our talent. So what better way than by trying to break into the movie and television industry?

We were doing a martial arts demo in Las Vegas and met this producer, Sally Baker. We eventually signed with her and she teamed up with Berry Gordy's Motown television and film division and Walt Disney Productions. As we were in the process of making projects happen, Ernie Jr. landed a part in Dino DeLaurentes' movie *Red Sonja* with Brigette Nelson and Arnold Schwarzenegger. I can remember the day when we got the call that we would be going to Italy for three months to make the film. Ernie Jr. and I took a moment and got down on our knees and said a prayer of thanks, feeling we were blessed in creating this extraordinary opportunity.

We had one of the biggest talent agencies representing both Ernie Jr. and me, called ICM. Michael Eisner was head of ABC, Michael Katzenberg was a head executive at Disney, and Michael Wisebarth and Susan DePasse were executives of Motown. With this team, they created a television series for us called *Side Kicks!* Ernie Jr., our West Coast Demo team members, and myself were also in a movie titled *Last Dragon*, a Motown production. At this time we felt that we had achieved success because we felt that we had accomplished something that was impossible.

It definitely was a gradual process and didn't happen overnight. It took indomitable spirit from Ernie Jr. and me to keep on going, and from all of the West Coast Team members, Master Tony Thompson, Donna Bernardi, Margie Betke, and all of the leaders of our association to keep the schools going back home to support us. It was the process of years of hard work, dedication, and massive hours of training early in the morning to get to this level. The sacrifice of moving to Hollywood with little financial means was challenging. We lived in a garage behind our aunt's house in a lower income part of Los Angeles just to make it. The success we felt at this time was all about our team and family unity! Our success system gave us an opportunity to give more exposure to the general public about martial arts entertainment and the positive life skills of martial arts training.

Attaining a certain level of success has made me extremely grateful. I feel very fortunate to have discovered one of the treasures of life and that is martial arts. I know that martial arts has the magic to change and empower people's lives! Every six months during our black belt test, I see for myself how our West Coast World Martial Arts Association system of martial arts has the power to bring together people of all ages, colors, races, and creeds, all coming together in peace and harmony because of the commonality of martial arts. This is the ultimate success goal! We all are making a difference in the world. My goals, my profession, and my life are all based on giving back to martial arts and creating a better world for all of us to live in through teaching the martial arts spirit.

Without martial arts, I just would have never, ever been able to become who I am today or done what I have accomplished and experienced. Some of the experiences during my lifetime are for others only dreams of opportunities that they would have loved to live. These dreams have become my reality. Just sharing my thoughts, philosophies, beliefs, values, and experiences during my lifetime, and reflecting on what success means to me for this book, made me really realize how lucky I have been to have martial arts as my way of life. Martial arts has empowered me to achieve goals from my wildest dreams that I never thought would be possible. I have had the opportunity to travel the world with my World Action Demo Team and Reyes family. We have brought smiles and joy all over the world! Martial Arts has taught me self-respect, self-discipline, to care for others, and to develop an indomitable spirit to never quit!

I am sixty-three years old, and somehow I have maintained a white belt mindset! It just seems like I have so much more to learn. I have been studying martial arts for forty-four years and I still feel like a beginner at times. I also have never forgotten the humble beginnings and roots of where I came from. My mom and dad, Valentina and Ernesto Reyes, were some of the first Filipino immigrants to ever come to America. They earned a few cents an hour and had to hold down two jobs just to survive. When I evaluate my life and the opportunities I have and compare it to what they had to overcome, their spirit is always with me to keep me going, growing, and training! I believe that martial arts is one of the greatest gifts to change people's lives for the better—physically, mentally and spiritually. In order to teach its benefits and empower people's lives, you must continue to grow and live it!

Master Reyes recommends:

Tao of Jeet Kune Do by Bruce Lee
Personal Power by Anthony Robbins
Think and Grow Rich by Napoleon Hill

It's Great to be You by Ray Saint
Good to Great by Jim Collins
Think Like a Champion by Donald Trump
Showing Up for Life by Bill Gates
Make Today Count by John Maxwell
Million Dollar Habits by Brian Tracy
The Secret by Rhonda Byrne
Body for Life by Bill Philips

SOLOMON'S WISDOM

Success requires passion. With passion you'll be able to overcome even the most challenging of obstacles.

Ernie Reyes is a world-class martial arts competitor and champion, developing seven national champions in one year, including his son Ernie Reyes, Jr., who at age eight was the youngest martial artist in history to be rated in the professional forms division. He was inducted into the Black Belt Hall of Fame by Black Belt Magazine. His West Coast World Action Team, which has traveled worldwide, was called the number one martial arts demo team in the world by Bushido Magazine in Europe. The team is still performing over thirty years later. He and his son, Ernie Jr. were represented by one of the biggest talent agencies in Los Angeles, ICM, and became part of Berry Gordy's Motown television and film division and Walt Disney Productions. The father-son team did demos and auditions at ABC, NBC, and CBS, which eventually led to a television series on ABC called Side Kicks! They recently completed an independent film called Red Canvas starring all of the Reyes children and his soul mate, Margie Betke.

OBSERVING YOUR WORLD TO ACHIEVE SUCCESS

Master Rondy McKee

Success is usually associated with money. For the most part, money does provide us with the things we need in order to feel successful: a nice place to live in a secure neighborhood, safe vehicles, preventative healthcare, good nutrition, fashionable styling, good education, and security for our future and the future of our heirs. For me, actually making the money—earning the money—or the ability to do so, defines success, rather than just having money. The sense of achievement is what truly fulfills me and gives my life purpose.

So what was my great accomplishment? Let me tell you all about it. If it sounds like I'm bragging, I am. I'm very proud. I live, eat, and breathe martial arts. I think it is the greatest activity on this earth, and all who participate benefit physically, mentally, and spiritually. The more people who I can get to train in the arts, the better a world it will be. To accommodate the masses of students I intend to teach in my lifetime, I built the world's largest martial arts school—White Tiger Taekwondo & Martial Arts. It is 24,000 square feet, has four training areas, supervised child-care, a fully equipped gym, a running track, showers, saunas, Swain mats throughout, a full kitchen, laundry, etcetera. There is a Koi pond in the cafe area, a rare and exotic orchid collection, state-of-the-art training equipment, and an incredible air filtration system. The fact that I spared no expense continually attracts new students. All classes are taught by members of the former Korean Tiger Team (Korea's Professional Martial Arts Team). The world-class curriculum and the phenomenal instruction keep the students motivated, and attrition low.

A small martial arts school owner called me lately. This master has been teaching for the past fifteen years, and has been unsuccessful. By unsuccessful, I mean that he is unfulfilled with the things he has accomplished. At approximately forty active students, I imagine that he does not have money either.

This master has repeatedly asked for my advice over the years. I am always happy to help, but every time I offer advice or recommend an idea that has proved successful for me in the past, he always has a reason as to why it would not possible work for him, in his city, in his location. He said to me, "You are just successful because you are so lucky." When I asked him to explain lucky, he replied, "You picked the right location with the right instructors in the right city at the right time. Everything has been so easy for you. It's not fair."

I told him that if I were that lucky, I would have picked the right numbers on the right day for the right lottery.

"Tell me things that you did in your life to get where you are now," he demanded. It was a great request, and really made me think back about the choices and observations that I have made in my life to become the person I am now. Most of these discoveries were made before I was old enough to attend high school. I think my childhood experiences were generally the same as anyone else has had. I was able to extract the importance from an event and catalog it away for later use.

Observation #1: Have a plan.

As a child, I remember having a vivid dream of being in a beautiful city building. In the dream, I could see the front wall of windows and actually feel the sun shining through and warming my skin. The floors were gray marble. There were many people bustling around, and you would think all of the clicking of footsteps would be noisy, but strangely ... it was peaceful; I heard nothing. I remember feeling a sense of pride—and knowing that I belonged there. It was like the feeling you get (women get) when you see Mary Tyler Moore throw her hat up into the air at the beginning of her show. Maybe I did get the idea from something on TV, because I lived in a very small town without such buildings. Even then, my mother did not drive, so we did not go to town that often. I told my mom one night that I wanted to have a big office. "You'd better plan to go to college," she said.

I said, "Okay, I plan to go to college."

Rephrasing, she said, "You'd better save your money to go to college. My job is to raise you until you are eighteen, and then you are on your own."

She was probably joking. But I was seven, and the way I saw it, I only had eleven years left to make some serious money.

Mom discussed it with Dad, and when he came home from work one day, they drove me to the bank in town. I had saved money from birthdays and Christmases, and I used it to open my savings account. I got a booklet to record my deposits.

Observation #2: Mind over matter

When I was young, I started having intense pains in the chest. The pain was so sharp that I would gasp for air but then be afraid to take in another breath. My body would just freeze up. I did not know this wasn't normal until my parents witnessed me "freezing up" and rolling out of my chair at the dinner table. When I was a kid, every pain was a "growing pain," and we were told to stop whining or they would give us something to cry about. All attention disorders were cured with a "boot in the ass." My parents sensed that this was more serious, and the next thing I knew I was in a hospital with goop on my chest and wires stuck to me. The EKG machine was not nearly as scary as the doctor who talked through a hole in his throat. Once I figured out that he was not a robot, but that he had something very wrong with his throat and voice, I listened to what he was telling me. He explained that I had the power to blink my eyes at will, the power to hold my breath or breathe. He showed me the lines on the monitor and asked me to concentrate on controlling my heartbeat. I studied the monitor while I concentrated with all my will to regulate my heart. The movement on the monitor gave me instant feedback, and I realized that my mind did have some power to control this function. Over the years I "outgrew" my heart condition and no longer needed to go for EKG checkups. I learned to finely hone this "mind over matter" technique to accomplish many things. When you operate your own business, especially when building your business, there are days when you just cannot be sick, injured, or under-the-weather. "I just don't have time for this," becomes very real. Our power over our minds needs to eliminate or at least postpone down days around our work schedules.

Observation #3: Recognizing opportunity and acting upon it.

My first go at my own business happened when I was in second grade. I had shown artistic talent and had been selected out of my class to work independently with the art teacher in a "special art" program. I was always making crafty and artsy things. My sister was the jock. At home (before the days of video games or even Pong) you could always find me tucked away in my bedroom making art things. I was constantly being interrupted by my mother to let her sewing clients try on their clothes in my room so that she could pin them. My mother was a housewife, but she did sewing alterations out of our house for pocket money. I would have to come out of my room, wait until they tried on the clothes, come out again while they tried on something else. It was non-stop traffic. "What 'cha makin'?" They would always ask. Hmm ... heavy traffic in and out of my room, people with money in hand, already expecting to pay for something, apparently interested in what I'm making.

The next sewing client came into my store to try his clothes on. I had taken my artsy bread dough art figures, attached them to pieces of old barn wood, and attached a beer can tab on the back for a hanger. I had taken down the giant yarn macramé owl from my bedroom and replaced it with lots of little nails. All of my artwork could be displayed with a price tag on every one. "Well, that will be $4 for the hemming of the pants and $5 for the mushroom plaque." It was all too easy. But Mom had another lesson to teach me not too far off in the future.

Observation #4: It does not matter how much you make, it's how much you keep.

"You can buy the next bag of flour," my mom informed me. What? I was rolling in the dough. A young kid trying to peddle his wares is too much for anyone to pass up. I was not only selling from my display wall, I was taking orders. It was a little dose of reality when mom informed me that I did not get to keep all of the money I was making. I had to start buying my own flour, shellac, paints, and etcetera. Luckily, my parents supplied me with an endless number of beer tabs. I figured out that I was making money, so I could buy the supplies to make the money.

Observation #5: Only take what you deserve.

My sister and I spent summers with my grandmother in Sault Ste. Marie. She let us go see the locks, eat lots of fudge, and dress up like Indians wearing beaded jewelry and fringe-cut tan garbage bags. On Sunday we went to church. Lots of church—Sunday school, talking to everyone, then the big church. It was never-ending until lunchtime. After lunch all of the grandmas would go out to this little fish restaurant out in the woods. This was the best part of the day. It wasn't the fish we liked; it was the fact that as soon as we finished eating, we were allowed to go outside and play with Jenny, the restaurant owner's daughter. Jenny had a big pile of old tires to play in—hours of fun right there. But, in addition, Jenny had a wildcat assortment that she had acquired from feeding scraps of fish leftovers. Wildcats and a pile o' dirty rainwater filled tires. Grandmas would talk for hours; the world was ours!

Just as my sister and I had pushed our food around enough to make it look as though we had eaten, we said that we would have a quick dessert so that we could be excused to go outside and play. My sister and I each grabbed for a packet of sugar from the table with plans to tear off the tops and pour them into our mouths. "You shouldn't steal; it's a sin."

Well, that didn't take long, I thought. I spent the whole morning getting cleansed from my sins and I'm dirty again already.

My grandmother, who to the best of my knowledge was a grandmother and not a philosopher or businesswoman, told me something that molded my character. If she would have stopped with "It's a sin; don't do it," it may or may not have had such an impact. But Grandma explained how the whole world is connected. She said, "The sugar packets are for customers who buy coffee. Those customers are entitled to or deserve a sugar packet. If people take sugar without paying for it by buying coffee, then Jenny's parents will have to spend their own money to buy more sugar packets for customers who buy coffee in the future. If they spend all of their money on buying extra supplies such as sugar, they will have less money to spend on Jenny. Maybe they cannot afford to buy Jenny new school clothes this year." I was old enough to understand that if Jenny had a pile of tires for a swing set, chances are that her parents did not have a lot of extra money, anyway. I vowed to never take anything that I did not deserve again.

Observation #6: Observe situations from all sides.

On a road trip with my parents to Michigan's upper peninsula, we had plenty of time for car watching and talking. My father worked for GM and was very proud of his product. If you did not drive a GM, then you didn't even think about parking in his driveway. As the hours passed, I kept noticing that all of the really old-looking pickup trucks (my father was on the truck line) that we saw on the road were Fords. I was quite impressed with my attention to detail. Such an observant mind I had. I needed to announce my discovery. I decided to get a few extra brownie points with my father. I piped up, "GM must make much better trucks than Ford, because all of the old Ford trucks driving on the road are old and beat-up looking."

My mother looked at me and said, "Maybe that's because all of the old GM trucks don't run anymore." I guess Mom was not after brownie points on that day. But what she said stopped me in my tracks. How could I have jumped to my conclusion while someone else with the same information (sights) came to another? What seemed so simple and obvious one moment became questionable the next. I learned to ask opinions of others and consider all sides before assuming answers and solutions.

Observation #7: Determination, perseverance and reliability will bring you farther than money, brains, or looks.

I was going to go to college and I felt I needed to speed up the learning process. In third grade, I asked my teacher if I could take home my math book over Christmas break. She was reluctant at first, warning me that I might lose it. I explained that my family was not traveling, and I promised to keep it safe. Our math books had a lesson a day for each day of the year. I wanted to get this third grade math out of the way. During my break, I disappeared into my room and went to work on finishing up the rest of the pages. Mom would interrupt me now and then to tell me to "go play outside and get some fresh air." We never had to stay outside too long. This was back before Thinsulate and waterproof gear; the insulation in our boots was made out of compressed dryer lint. Soon our little bodies would stiffen up, and mom would reel us back inside. I would get right back to work. On our first day back to school, I was confused by the look on my teacher's face when I handed her the tall stack of papers. "Finished it." She talked to a lot of other teachers that day. I knew that they were talking about me. The next day my teacher explained to me that I was getting a new book. When it was time for math every day, I was to walk down the hall to the fourth grade classes. I was to learn the lesson for the day with Mr. Kay's fourth grade class, and then was return back to my class. I loved it. I asked permission to take home other books. I needed to be moved up in other subjects as well. There were timing conflicts with some subjects, and I was asked if I minded missing recess so that I could attend. Getting a chance to miss recess was like a gift from God. I did not need recess time to be reminded that I was the slowest, most unathletic, and last to be picked for every team. (Taekwondo would not be introduced into my life until much later.)

Soon I was running out of things to do. My mother was evolving as well. She got a driver's license and starting taking night art classes at the community adult education program downtown. She enjoyed the freedom of driving, but the classes seemed a little more than she wanted to do. She was talking about being disappointed because she had paid for the class but did not want to take it. "I'll take it in your place!" We got permission initially for me to take the first class—I suspect because they did not want to issue a refund. I behaved and was a good student, so I was allowed to take many more. I took all of the art classes I could: sculpting, drawing, painting, calligraphy, etcetera. Back in regular school, once in sixth grade, there was little for me to do. I was still working with the art teacher in a special arts program, but had finished all of the textbooks for my grade. Seventh grade was middle school and it was taught in another building across town, so there would be no more moving classrooms. I was asked if I wanted to become Mrs. C.'s assistant. Mrs. C. taught kindergarten. I accepted. I learned how to instruct a class, keep the attention, and motivate the little guys to learn. I loved it. I may have only been eleven years old, but I was much older than my students, and they looked up to me.

I was perhaps an above-average student in my academic studies but was far from the smartest in my class. I was a good artist, but not exactly someone with mind-blowing talent. It really was an intense determination, perseverance, and reliability in all of my work that gave me opportunities before anyone else.

College was a disappointment. I had taken so many extra art classes, already had teaching experience, and had taken on years of freelance advertising and marketing projects. I just did not feel the professors had anything new to offer me. I took my classes by the "directed study" method, where I could go at my own pace and test out when I completed the lesson. I finished all my classes early and used the remainder of the semester to work on freelance projects through several instructors.

I was offered a job in my field early and left college after the first year. I figured I could spend money for the next three years of school, or I could begin making money immediately. I opened my own advertising agency by the age of twenty.

Observation #8: Be flexible.

I grew up in rural Michigan. Our yard was 3.25 acres. We had 103 trees in our yard, or at least in the part of the yard where we cut the grass. I am sure of these numbers, because it was the chore of my sister and me to take care of the yard. Even when we were too little to use the lawnmower, we were big enough to trim around the 103 trees. This was before we had weed whackers. This was before we had scissors with comfy soft stuff on the handles. I had the big metal-handled righty scissors, and my sister had the big metal-handled lefties. Out in the country, there were a lot of fields between the houses. Down the road lived our closest neighbor. They had one tree in their yard. Unlike the big majestic oak trees in our yard, they had a solo weeping willow.

In the spring, Michigan is prone to intense storms and tornadoes. There are lots of snow and ice storms in the fall and winter. (I moved as soon as I was old enough). Dragging a blanket, flashlight, portable TV, and the pets down the basement to wait out the storm was a regular part of our routine. After a storm, our yard would be a mess. The strong unyielding trees in our yard would snap and break under the stress. Unwilling to bend, the great trees would lose their top and, with it, their leaves. Smaller trees, once stunted by the greater tree's shade would take advantage of the access to sunlight and shoot up toward the sky. Huge trees that had withstood for decades could be taken out overnight by a strong gust of wind.

In our neighbor's yard, the weeping willow stood. I recall watching the tree's branches blow almost completely sideways, as

I watched from their basement during a storm. In the winter, the ice or snow would weigh on the branches, flexing all the way down to the ground. Once the winds died down, once the ice thawed, the willow would always spring back up, ready for action. Its flexibility, often perceived as a weakness, was actually it's strength.

In business we can anticipate and prepare for storms. But just like weather, you are never exactly sure when, where, and how severely you are going to get hit. Our country and the world are currently in a recession. I own a martial arts school. Food, shelter, medical care, etcetera are all necessities, but for many families, martial arts may not be. My business has been moved from fulfilling the "extracurricular activities" budget, to being possibly cut from the budget entirely. But, I have forty-two employees that need to provide food, shelter, medical care, and etcetera for their families, so I must find a way to weather the storm.

The rigid discipline and strict rules of a traditional martial arts school, normally its strength, can become its weakness if flexibility cannot be found in changing times. "This is a black belt school" and "we sell only three-year contracts" will not fly in times when people do not know whether they will have a job tomorrow. Consumer's concerns and minds are now different; businesses must be able to be flexible and make adjustments to accommodate. White Tiger now offers month-by-month membership options, more martial art/childcare combination programs, and even a program that offers training only one time per week at a reduced rate, fitting consumers' "reduced" budgets.

At the same time, we are mindful to preserve the quality of the program and the level of instruction—just being more patient for results. After all, it is the journey and not the destination that is truly important for the martial artist.

As the wind blows, we will flex and bend. There may even be a little weeping. Our roots are deep; proper investments have been made. When the storm finally blows over, we will stand upright, ready for new growth. Our schooling can educate us, our parents and mentors can guide us, books can inform us, but we are our own best teachers. Observe the life around you, and learn the lessons within it.

This life training enabled me to recognize the time to move on from my studies. I had my first art director position at an agency as a teenager. This is when I discovered martial arts. Working late at night in the city, especially in Detroit, is not a good idea for a little girl. It soon became obvious that some form of self-protection/defense would be needed. Gradually, I found more value in teaching others the benefits of martial arts than I did in promoting consumer goods. The martial artist in me won out over the commercial artist in me. Using my same basic philosophies that were rooted in my childhood, I applied myself at a deeper level into the martial arts. A partnership in a martial arts school eventually led to a position on the world-famous Korean Tiger Professional Martial Arts Team. I packed my bags, sold my belongings, passed my accounts on to employees, and moved to South Korea. As a member of this traveling team, I had the opportunity to observe the elite-level schools that hosted us. Realizing that only a successful school could afford to host such a team, I studied and looked for the common denominator.

I planned to move back to the States and bring the world's best martial artists to a facility in which other Americans could train.

I kept a strong mind. Every master including my own told me that a school with multiple masters taking direction from an American manager would never work. "Americans don't need and won't appreciate this level of training," I was told.

I watched for the opportunity. I studied locations of famous/large schools in America and found a hole between heavily Korean-populated Washington DC and the successful franchise schools of the more southern states. I called a realtor from Korea and explained what sort of lease space I was looking for. I asked him to find ten locations that fit my description. I picked the fourth one that I looked at.

I realized that I had more time than money, and also knew that it was important to save as much as possible of the limited money I had. I did everything that I could do myself—from the architectural build-out drawings to the photography and writing of the instructional manual. All signage was hand cut and assembled "craft style." Anything that I did not know how to do, I read up on.

I took what I deserved. When Master Chang's father was told that I was moving back to America and planned to take his son with me, he was not pleased. He understood that I planned to make a school and had my mind set. He tried to entice me to stay in Korea with an offer. When I arrived in his house, there was a pile of money on the living room floor. By a pile, I really mean a pile. The largest paper bill in Korea was worth around thirteen American dollars. I was told there was over $200,000 in the pile. The money was meant for me to stay in Korea and make a business or whatever I wanted, just as long as I did not take his son away. But I did not deserve that money. I did nothing to earn it. I graciously declined his offer and apologized for stealing his son, but promised to make his son successful beyond his wildest dreams.

I observed my operating procedures from all sides. I knew what it was like to be a paying student of the martial arts and also knew what it was like to manage a school. No longer with support of any master, I was free from the traditional ways. I was able to iron out all the wrinkles that I felt that were unfair or "not quite right" in the system. I designed a system that allowed for the traditional Korean culture feel, while catering to the customer as Americans are accustomed.

Once the school opened, I learned the real meaning of determination and perseverance. While I was touring with the Korean Tigers, I had the opportunity to pick the brains of our host masters. A master's wife wished me luck with the new school. She also told me to be prepared to cry every day for the first three months. I laughed. I am not laughing now. She was right; the first few months were not only physically exhausting, they wore me down mentally as well. The only thing more stressful than having too many students coming at once is have none come at all. But we consistently taught great classes, and eventually the flow evened out.

The observation to be flexible was used in the beginning when dealing with the planning committee, the builders, inspectors, and etcetera. Now with Korean and American employees, everyone has to be flexible. White Tiger has become a small community where two (and more) different cultures have to co-exist and be productive. It is my nature to run my business in the clear-cut rules and laws that our society provides. But a "too American" culture is uncomfortable for many Koreans, and if they are not comfortable, I run the risk of them going back home. I constantly remind myself to be flexible with an open mind so that I, too, can weather blows from any direction.

Following my own observations, the school flourished. After three years in that location, we had outgrown our space. Weighing our options and the need to invest led us to begin the process of building our own facility.

White Tiger fills me with a sense of pride, accomplishment, and financial security. I had to go through a few realtors to find a location where I could build facing the proper way for the sun to shine through the windows just right. Real marble is too slippery, so I hand painted the floors to look like gray marble with tiger stripes around the perimeter. With 2,500 active students, their families, and their friends, the place is always bustling. The belt color-coded cubbies neatly store the shoes, respecting Korean culture. I remember my dream of my own building from long ago in which the students' bare feet on the floor make no sound.

As I enjoy my life in my school, I often look down at my belt. Once black, the material has "weathered" and faded to gray. The threads have worn and the inner white fabric is exposed in many places. The black belt, the symbol of my status and experience is coming around full circle, returning to white. The white belt: the blank canvas, unlimited potential representing a beginner student of martial arts. New life.

My personal dreams of success have been planned, strived for, weathered through, and fulfilled.

A parent experiences a deeper meaning of life and greater joy through the experiences of her own child. As a master or mentor, I can only imagine my greater sense of accomplishment coming from guiding others to achieve success of their own. I share my observations, my experience, and my proven techniques in hopes that others, too, can be accused of being lucky.

SOLOMON'S WISDOM:
When you see opportunity, take it.

Master Rondy holds multiple black belts in various martial arts disciplines including a Seventh Degree Black Belt in Taekwondo and a Fifth Degree Black Belt Hapkido. She is the owner and program director of White Tiger Taekwondo and Martial Arts, the largest martial arts school in North America. Master Rondy lived, trained, and taught in South Korea for two years and was the only Caucasian member of the Korean Tiger Professional Demonstration Team.

Master Rondy is a columnist for Taekwondo Times Magazine, blending the best of the Korean and American cultures in "East meets West."

She is the Founder of the award-winning White Tiger Community Cares Program benefiting at-risk youth, working with the local police department toward youth gang avoidance.

For more information on White Tiger Taekwondo and Martial Arts or on White Tiger MD-Management Development, mentoring service for martial arts schools, visit www.WhiteTigerTKD.com or MasterRondy@aol.com

OVERCOMING OBSTACLES

Bill Wallace

The most important thing that any person can do to achieve success is to find something that you love and that you have fun doing. Even after all of the years that I have spent training, I still love sparring. It still provides a challenge.

In addition to finding something you love, it also helps if it's something you're good at and for which you have some natural ability to begin with. In college I wanted to be a boxer, but I wasn't so great. I came to realize that I was a much better fighter than boxer. Find out if you are compatible with what you do and what you want to achieve. Sometimes you have to rearrange your priorities.

This idea of pursuing what your natural abilities seem to dictate is practiced in Russian schools, where they test children at a young age to see what skills they exhibit in order to train them in those skills. Working to hone and develop skills that you already have is a lot easier than starting from scratch.

For me, success is equivalent with winning. You can't win if you don't have or develop the right skills. To succeed, a business-person has to be aggressive, go after clients, go after businesses, and he can't be afraid to do what he needs to do. A boxer doesn't like getting hit. I hated getting hit. I worked very hard at not getting hit. If a boxer doesn't have a good defense, chances are that he's not going to win very often. Defense is very important.

If at the end of a fight only one punch made contact, who is going to win the fight? You would say that person who threw that one punch, right? But if at the end of the fight, one fighter got in thirty-five punches and the other got in thirty-four, who wins? Now you have to look at who hit hardest, who had better form, who looked better, and all of these other factors that affect a fighter's success. All of the power in the world doesn't count if you don't get a hit.

The same goes for achieving success. You can be the most driven person out there, determined to accomplish your goal, but if you don't have the abilities necessary to back up that determi-nation, you are not going to be successful. In a fight, you have to have ability and finesse. If I'm good, quick, and strong I can win against any opponent.

Your mental ability—what goes on in those four inches between your ears—is most important. Take golf, for example. In golf you use the same swing every time. You use the same muscles, the same tools, and the same environment. What changes is what goes on in your head, your state of mind—and that is what makes all the difference.

You have to know your own worth, especially when you're up against an intimidating opponent. If I know that I'm better than you are, I'm not going to let you beat me. If you want to beat me, you'll have to kill me. Don't quit when the going gets tough. Use that as an opportunity to test your strength.

It's important to know your weaknesses as well as your strengths. Everyone is going to lose a couple of battles in the attempt to win the war. If you know what you're doing wrong, you can correct it. Don't be overcome by mental or physical disabilities; work to overcome them. It's important to learn from your mistakes. If you fail, ask yourself why.

If you are running a business, what is it that you are offering people? What are you selling? What do people want? How does your product or service meet that need? We see this example in some major corporations. Take Starbucks for example. At the time when Starbucks was emerging and growing in popularity, everyone wanted coffee. There was a need for a local coffee house, a gathering place, etcetera. Starbucks filled that need.

If you win, you feel great, because you got everything you wanted. If you don't win, figure out why and correct your mistakes. This might take more than one attempt. You might come up with the wrong solution to correct a problem. You have to keep changing, keep reevaluating, and keep readjusting. If something doesn't work, don't hold on to it. Change it. When I kick and someone blocks it, the first thing I want to find out is how they did it so that I can make sure it never happens again. You have to correct your mistakes. Doing something wrong over and over again isn't going to make you any better.

Even if there's nothing inherently wrong with the way you're doing something, there is always a better way to do it. The way you decide to do something might work better for you than the way someone taught you to do it. You should always change and modify things to make them better. You have to decide what works best for you and what makes you the most effective.

If you were in a situation in which you needed to use a self-defense technique from your martial arts training, you would use whichever technique came to mind first. This may only be around three to five—or even less—of all of the techniques you have ever learned. That's because these are the most comfortable for you, the most familiar, the techniques that work best for you.

The only way to achieve success is to do things right now instead of putting them off. It's about having the right attitude, a do-it-now attitude. It's too easy to keep putting things off, and it hinders you from doing what you really want to do. You have to go for it: take every opportunity and don't waste a second of your precious time. It's easy to say, "Oh, I'll do it next time." But what if there is no next time?

You've got to push for what you want. If a businessman goes in for a meeting with a fifteen-million-dollar client wearing short sleeves with his shirt untucked and his pants all wrinkled, he is showing that client that he doesn't care. He isn't doing everything in his power to get what he wants. This is why it's important to do something that you love. If you love doing it, it doesn't become a burden or a chore to put in that extra effort. You do it because it's fun. Lawyers have fun. They argue, they call each other bad names, and then they go out and get a drink together. To them, it's all a game.

I feel that I have had a very successful career. I have done everything I wanted to do in my chosen field. However, I have had failures, and I have had to make sacrifices. My failure is as a father and a husband. I wasn't there when my kids needed me, and I left my wife. It hurts like hell knowing that I wasn't there to see them grow up, but at least it's nice to know that they still love me and have my name. What I have learned from this failure is to never quit. I quit on them, and I never want to make that same mistake again. If I'm going to do something, I'm going all the way.

It's important to remember that one person can't do everything. Everyone needs help at some point. I have friends in the martial arts field who have helped me succeed. What I can't do, they can do, and vice versa. We're all in this together, so we all help each other out. Don't be afraid to ask for help when you need it, and certainly don't hesitate to give help to those who ask for it.

I travel a lot, which prevents me from being around any set group of individuals all the time. When I'm fighting, I am alone. I get all the glory or all the fault, and I have to be able to accept that. No one can help me win. Yes, they can help me train and prepare, but when it comes down to it, no one is in control of winning except me.

The mark of a successful person is happiness. You can't take money with you; love is fleeting; but even if you are happy for fifteen minutes, that is a success. I never had a nine-to-five job. I've always done martial arts. It wasn't difficult for me to achieve success, because I am flexible, fast, and have a do-it-now attitude. I loved martial arts when I started, and I still do now.

Even after my success, I still continue to train. I am sixty-three years old. I'm not going to become faster, stronger, or smarter. I've got to maintain. Now I like to do seminars to provide ideas for students about improving flexibility, speed, agility, power, and the way they think, in order to pass on what I have learned about reaching their goals.

Books by Bill Wallace:
Karate: Basic Concepts and Skills
Dynamic Kicking and Stretching
The Ultimate Kick

SOLOMON'S WISDOM:
For most of the authors in this book, becoming successful was more of a mental journey. For Mr. Wallace, so much of his success was hard physical work. Combining the two is a great message.

Bill "Superfoot" Wallace retired as the undefeated Professional Karate Association (PKA) Middleweight Champion after defeating Bill Biggs in a twelve-round bout in June 1980. The twenty-third straight victory signaled the end to an illustrious fifteen-year career in tournament and full-contact fighting. Known to the karate world simply as "Superfoot," symbolic of his awesome left leg, which was once clocked in excess of 60 mph, Superfoot left a string of battered and bruised bodies along the martial arts fighting trail. He used his foot as others would use their hands, faking opponents with two or three rapid fake kicks and following with one solid knockout technique. His power was amazing, his precision astounding. Superfoot, a five-foot ten-and-a-half-inch native of Portland, Indiana, began studying karate in February 1967 after suffering a right leg injury in a judo accident. The injury left him without the use of the leg in karate competition. Some observers said that Superfoot was committing martial arts suicide. He, however, had other ideas. In the next seven years Superfoot, named after an advertisement for a "super-foot-long hot dog", dominated the point-tournament circuit.

As a national champion point fighter three years in a row, Superfoot captured virtually every major event on the tournament circuit. The more prestigious victories included: the U.S. Championships (three times), the USKA Grand Nationals (three times), and the Top Ten Nationals (two times). He was such a dominant figure in martial arts that Black Belt Magazine, the bible of industry publications, named him to its Hall of Fame three times in seven years—twice as "Competitor of the Year" and once as "Man of the Year."

In 1973, Superfoot, whose education includes a bachelor's degree (1971) in physical education from Ball State University and a master's degree (1976) in kinesiology (the study of human movement) from Memphis State University, suffered what many considered a career-ending injury. However, one of Superfoot's *friends, the late Elvis Presley, flew in a Los Angeles acupuncturist to treat the karate champion at Graceland Manor.*

A year later, he turned professional and captured the PKA middleweight karate championship with a second-round knock-out (hook kick) of West German Bernd Grothe in Los Angeles. He relinquished the crown in 1980, undefeated and respected around the world.

Despite his retirement, Superfoot continues to be one of the martial arts most popular figures. He is the author of three books: Karate: Basic Concepts & Skills, Dynamic Kicking & Stretching, and The Ultimate Kick.

As well as a former member of the President's Council on Physical Fitness, Wallace also has been active in the film industry.

His credits include: A Force of One with Chuck Norris; Kill Point with Cameron Mitchell; Continental Divide and Neighbors with John Belushi, for whom he acted as trainer and bodyguard; Protector with Jackie Chan; A Prayer for the Dying with Mickey Rourke, Ninja Turf; and A Sword of Heaven.

To schedule a seminar or for more information please call 727.224.3496

TURNING FEAR INTO OPPORTUNITIES

Omar Periu

"If you don't hear opportunity knocking, find another door."
Omar Periu

Every fiber of my small, seven-year-old body was fearfully shaking as we walked through customs and I heard my pregnant mother explain, as I clung to her dress, the purpose of our trip: "We are vacationing in Miami." Even though my mother said those words, I knew that we would never be going home again. Communism was quickly tightening the noose around the free enterprise system in Cuba, and my father, who was a successful entrepreneur, decided that it was time to take his family and flee to a land where freedom, promise, and opportunity were alive and thriving. Looking back now, it was a very courageous decision that my parents made for us.

Castro's regime was watching my father very carefully, making it necessary for my mother to bring my brother and me over first; then my father met us a few weeks later. When I arrived at the Miami International Airport, I was very overwhelmed; everybody was speaking in strange words that did not make sense to me. We arrived with no money, had no family here, no friends. That's right; we arrived with nothing but the clothes on our backs!

Within a few months, we were on a church-sponsored flight to Joliet, Illinois, via Chicago's O'Hare International Airport. A burst of cold air greeted us as we walked out of the terminal into the still-talked-about winter of Chicago. It had snowed nearly four feet; this, too, was overwhelming as we had never felt cold air such as this. Amidst the blowing drifts stood a young priest waiting to take us to our new home. This was an absolutely amazing experience for a Cuban boy who had never seen snow.

My father is an educated man; he owned a chain of gas stations and a car dealership in Cuba. Although my father was unable to speak English, he adapted quickly and he found work as a mechanic. Thanks to St. Patrick's church, we were able to find a small but comfortable apartment in a middle-class neighborhood. We did not have a lot of material things; however, we had what mattered most—each other, a whole lot of love from my mother and father, and my father's burning desire to succeed.

Escaping communist Cuba with my parents instilled in me an incredible ability to use my fear, the ability to change it from my enemy to ally. My mother and father were determined to give me every opportunity to follow my dreams in America, even when it meant sacrificing everything to gain our freedom—and it did! If they could give so much, how could I let a little thing like fear stand in the way of my success? I began a journey as that small child—a journey of "becoming" that bridged countries, cultures, and customs. A journey dedicated to becoming the best!

It was during this time that my father, with his tattered Spanish copy of Dale Carnegie's book, *How to Win Friends and Influence People*, taught me one of the greatest lessons in life. He told me over and over again: "It doesn't matter who you are, where you're from, or what color you are. You can do anything you put your mind to." These words gave me comfort and inspiration as my brother and I mixed into the great Chicago melting pot. My brother Ed and I struggled in school. Because we couldn't speak English, it was not uncommon to be called a "spic," not to be chosen to be on a team, or have our hand-me-down bikes stolen, but my father's words continued to burn inside of me. We also met some truly wonderful people who helped us overcome the obstacles of adjusting to our new surroundings. Many of these people are still my best friends today.

It still wasn't easy—this "becoming." Not only did I look different and speak a different language, but I was also smaller, shyer, and, often, I felt alone. For months, my only companion was the monkey on my back—its name was fear! I couldn't ignore it and I didn't know how to overcome it, so I chose to learn from it. When my schoolmates picked on me because of my size, I built my body up and became one of the strongest, fastest, most agile athletes in my school, setting and holding records that still stand today. When I was teased because of my speech, I learned to speak clearly. When I was fourteen, my father was already teaching me about the great principle of free enterprise. He gave me $18 for every set of valves and engine heads that I would clean and grind (what we called a valve job). Later he taught me how to hire other people to do the work for me, and I went out and found new customers and collected money—basically ran the business. Little did I know that he was teaching me how to be an entrepreneur. America was truly a land of promise.

I was also fortunate to be born into a musically talented family. I remember listening to my mother sing beautiful Spanish songs to me as I was growing up. These songs inspired me to sing in the church choir as a boy soprano, and because of this influence, my brother Ed started a contemporary rock band. I attended every band rehearsal and at night harmonized with him and my mother. Later, through working as a laborer in a stone quarry and a scholarship, I studied opera and music at Southern Illinois University. After two years of college, I went back to work in the stone quarry and saved the money I earned for my move west to California. My goal in moving to California was to break into the music business and cut my own records. It did not take very long for reality to set in. I had to take a job selling health club memberships to support myself. Reality and depression set in. I was broke and did not know where to turn. Then I met Tom Murphy, one of the owners of the health club.

My father always told me that if you want to be wealthy, you have to do what wealthy people do, so I asked Mr. Murphy if we could talk over coffee to find out what made him so successful. It just so happened that Mr. Murphy was the business partner of Tom Hopkins, one of the country's top sales trainers. So, of course, he recommended that I start attending sales training seminars and I began reading self-improvement books and listening to sales tapes. He also introduced me to many successful business men and women and to their published materials. I was so hungry for success that it did not take long before I was the top salesperson in the company. But that wasn't good enough for me. After saving every penny I could, I invested in my own health club. By the time I was finished, I owned a chain of the most successful health clubs and sports medicine facilities in the United States, but I still had not achieved my goal—to cut my own record.

Recording my first demo was exciting yet discouraging, as I presented it to record company after record company. Each time I heard the word "no." Not to be defeated, I recorded the demo in Spanish and took it back to the same record companies—all with the same results. On the verge of giving up, I called my father to discuss what had happened. He said, "Omar, you're doing very well financially, aren't you?" I replied, "Yes, I am." "Well," my father said, *"why don't you just buy a record company and record your music?"* When I went back to the record company, I intended to buy, hoping to save my ego, I asked the company executives one more time to record my music. They said, *"Omar, we can't help you! Go to Broadway. You will be great there."* You should have seen their faces when I told them that I was going to be the new owner.

I then set out to finance, record and then produce my first album in Spanish. From there I went on to be named "Best Latin Male Vocalist" and "Entertainer of the Year" in 1986, 1987, and 1988. However, when you think that everything is going to be great from now on, life seems to throw a new challenge your way. My father, trying to get back to his aristocratic days in Cuba, was working seven days a week, eighteen-hour days. He had accumulated gas stations and an auto parts store—a ten-stall auto mechanic garage, a block worth of apartment buildings, and his own home. The stress was too much for him; he had a massive heart attack.

When I stood by my father's hospital bed as he fought for his life after suffering the massive heart attack, he lost his properties and business and everything that he had worked so hard to obtain. I once again listened to my fear and allowed it to strengthen me instead of overwhelm me. At a young age, I knew that I never wanted my family to experience that kind of loss again. That was another day of change. Now I was passionately driven to use my fear, making it my ally. I created the power with God as my pilot to help myself and others to reach our greatest potential in life.

That's what moves me and continues to move me to become one of today's most sought out motivational teachers. It's strange how the things that you go through not only make you stronger but also catapult you to encourage yourself and others to refuse to acknowledge or buy into their fears. Up until then I had wrestled with this self-defeating fear. Now I learned and created a system to defeat it and to bring about positive changes in my life and others. I had to realize that only I had the power to harness the fear and work with it instead of fighting against it; I gave it a voice and used it to fuel my passion on the road to success.

Now, my question to you is, what does your fear say to you? Does your fear tell you that you are inferior? Start your own journey to superiority! Does fear tell you that you can't? Prove to fear that you can by following your dreams, setting and accomplishing positive goals. Does fear whisper convenient excuses of why you haven't achieved that which you wish? Make a liar out of fear; instead of listening to the excuses for your professional and personal setbacks, commit yourself to travel your own road to excellence!

Here are three easy steps to harness and use the power of fear to make it your ally instead of your enemy! When fear would hold you back …

1. Perceive yourself as one who has already achieved greatness!
2. Believe that you can achieve your dreams and pursue them relentlessly!
3. Receive all of the blessings that life offers and celebrate your successes!

We have all been given fearfulness! I, for one, feel that it was provided as a tool to cause us to act instead of hide—to believe in our abilities to achieve instead of being paralyzed by mistaken beliefs. We have a choice of how we're going to journey to our final destination, and our happiness and fulfillment is created in whom, not what, we become during our travels. With fear as your ally instead of your enemy, your perception will be one of lifelong learning rather than lifelong yearning. However, there is more; you must master the power to control those thoughts.

Most people in life fail because of a lack of self-belief, not because of a lack of talent. Remember, what you think deep down, you are. Peak performers have learned to handle obstacles better than the average, because in life, it's not what you get, it's what you do with what you get that makes the difference.

Learn to make success work for you, by taking from the day, rather than going through the day. This means that every day you wake up with passion, fire, and desire. You wake up with intent, intent of what you want to achieve from the day. My mentors taught me that success locked in a vault is unused energy. Like energy, its value diminishes with time. I recommend that you immediately adopt this mentality to attract success to help you create the proper framework for nurturing, protecting, and growing that success.

Most of the barriers that block our way to success are self-imposed. Sure, some barriers can be out of our control. However, in those rare cases the *limitations* that we allow those barriers to impose most certainly are self-generated. They become one of those conditions. The conditions that we have programmed over time in our lives by primary experience help us to move either toward success or away from it. If there's one constant thought running throughout the wisdom of the ages, it is, "Our life is what our thoughts make it." Our real barriers and limitations come from within. So do our real strengths.

What happens in your life is a direct reflection of your thoughts. You become what you think about most. If you think positive thoughts most of the time, you will become a success. If you think negative thoughts most of the time, you will become disappointed, disillusioned, and quit whatever it is that you're trying to achieve. Feed your mind positive thoughts of wealth, success, achievement, and happiness, and your mind will work just as hard to make those things happen. It's an automatic process too-little understood and too-little used. "Change your thinking and you will change your life." Focus on zero and you will earn zero. Focus on success and wealth and you will inevitably achieve success and wealth.

People who set their minds on achievement will always make a successful journey. Circumstances, no matter how severe, will always be overcome. Challenges will be met, opportunities will be exploited. Believe that you can achieve great success. Find your purpose, plan your dreams, strategically execute them, create the daily rituals of successful people, and your will become a great success.

It's never a question of can you succeed, but it's always a question of will you succeed? Will you take the test to get the lesson? Meaning, the only way that you will learn what I teach is by internalizing it and using it so that you can learn, change, grow, improve and become, from the experience.

Remember: you have the ability, so never give up on your dreams—no matter what!

"Success is in the moment; make every moment count."

SOLOMON'S WISDOM

Don't let fear stand in your way of success.
Embrace your fear, and use it to make you stronger!

Omar Periu is a man of power whose life story is truly remarkable. Omar is more than a motivator; his peers refer to him as the "The Motivational Teacher." Possessing an indefinable quality of magnetism, Omar brings audiences to their feet. Although the terms "dynamic," "high energy," and "super achiever" all describe Omar Periu as he is today, they aren't exactly the words that portrayed the results accomplished early in his career.

Today, he is one of the nation's top success executives and trainers, promoting "how-to" tactics and strategies in his seminars throughout the world. Omar's content is fresh and inspiring, his presentations impeccable, and his story unforgettable. Omar is now referred to as the #1 Motivational Teacher in America, a world-traveled speaker who has spent over a decade educating salespeople, managers, and entrepreneurs worldwide. He has personally delivered more than five thousand seminars, workshops, and training programs. He has trained more than two million people in more than two-thirds of the Fortune 500 companies. He has been a featured speaker at events with superstars Zig Ziglar, Tony Robbins, Donald Trump, Robert Kyosaki, General Colin Powell, Tony Robbins, Larry Bird, Harvey Mackay, Jim Rohn, Terry Bradshaw, and Lou Holtz, among others. His articles are published in Success Magazine, Sales and Management Magazine, Selling Power Magazine, and many, many more. He is the author of today's #1 book in sales, Investigative Selling™. This year, he has been presented with the Business Man of the Year award for the State of Florida by the Florida Business Advisory Council. He is on the Board of Directors to Wayne Huizenga's School of Entrepreneurs and Nova Southeastern University.

He is a member of the National Speakers Association and has been inducted into the prestigious International Platform Association. Also, he is one of the four approved speakers in the world to train the U.S. Army on leadership and selling skills. Most importantly, he has dedicated himself to helping others fulfill their dreams by teaching them what his mentors taught him—how to achieve greatness!

To reach Omar Periu, e-mail success@omarperiu.com or go to his Web site www.omarperiu.com

To quote Omar's philosophy:

"Success is in the moment—make every moment count!"

DOUBLE YOUR RETENTION!!!

What are the two most important jobs in your school?

1. ENROLL NEW STUDENTS 2. KEEP THE OLD ONES

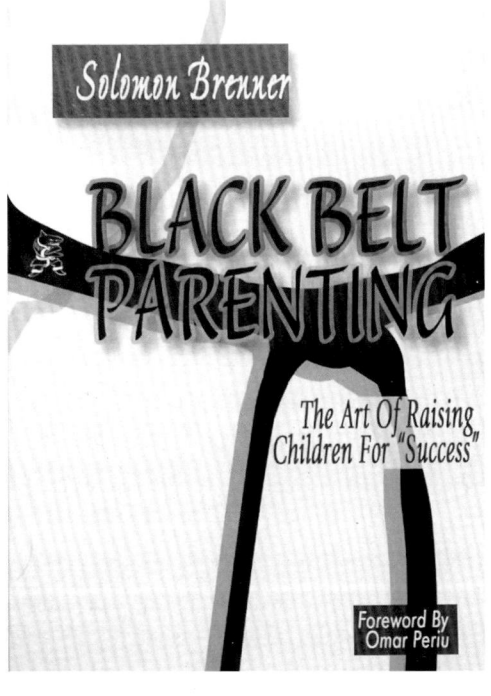

In his book, *Black Belt Parenting: The Art of Raising Children for Success*, Brenner speaks directly to your students' parents.

You may have asked yourself, "How can I get Mom or Dad to be my strongest advocate before a child wants to quit?" Black Belt Parenting arms the parents with what to do if their child wants to quit, including how to maintain a positive attitude throughout his or her training, rise to a challenge, be a good role model, and more. This non-style-specific book is one more retention tool to help you encourage families to commit to achieving their martial arts goals.

To order your copy of Black Belt Parenting
call 215-355-5003.
To include in your school's new student package,
ask about wholesale pricing

SPECIAL FREE GIFT FROM THE AUTHOR
E-mail the information below to ActionKarate@comcast.net

FREE
30-Minute "Take Your Business to the Next Level" Phone Consultation

Yes, Solomon I want to take my school to the next level and make a bigger impact in my community.

Name _____

School Name _____

Address _____

City/State/Zip_____

E-mail _____

Phone _____

Fax _____

Best time to call _____

ACTION TIPS

_____

_____

_____

_____

_____

_____

_____

_____

_____

_____

_____

_____

_____

_____

ACTION TIPS

ACTION TIPS

_____

_____

_____

_____

_____

_____

_____

_____

_____

_____

_____

_____

_____

_____

_____

ACTION TIPS

_____

_____

_____

_____

_____

_____

_____

_____

_____

_____

_____

_____

_____

_____

_____

ACTION TIPS

_____

_____

_____

_____

_____

_____

_____

_____

_____

_____

_____

_____

_____

_____

_____

ACTION TIPS

_____

_____

_____

_____

_____

_____

_____

_____

_____

_____

_____

_____

_____

_____

_____

ACTION TIPS
